BEGINNING *your new life* IN CHRIST

BEGINNING your new life IN CHRIST

MICHAEL GREEN

OLIVER
NELSON

THOMAS NELSON PUBLISHERS
Nashville • Atlanta • London • Vancouver

Published in Nashville, Tennessee, by Thomas Nelson, Inc., Publishers, and distributed in Canada by Word Communications, Ltd., Richmond, British Columbia.

Biblical quotations are the author's own rendering of the original Greek, unless otherwise specified. Verses marked TLB are taken from *The Living Bible,* copyright © 1971 by Tyndale House Publishers, Inc., Wheaton, IL. Used by permission. Scripture quotations noted NRSV are from The New Revised Standard Version of the Bible. Copyright © 1989 by the Division of Christian Education of the National Council of the Churches of Christ in the United States of America.

First published in Great Britain 1973 by Hodder and Stoughton Limited of Mill Road, Dunton Green, Sevenoaks, Kent, TN13 2YA, England. Original title: NEW LIFE, NEW LIFESTYLE. Previously published in the U.S. 1985 by Multnomah of 10209 Southeast Division Street, Portland, OR 97266.

Library of Congress Cataloging-in-Publication Data

Green, Michael, 1930–
    Beginning your new life in Christ / Michael Green.
      p. cm.
    Rev. ed. of: New life, new lifestyle. 1973.
    ISBN 0-7852-8190-8 (pbk.)
    1. Christian life—Anglican authors. 2. Conversion. I. Green, Michael, 1930– New life, new lifestyle. II. Title.
    BV4501.2.G7452   1994
    248.4´83—dc20   94-30533
                                                      CIP

Printed in the United States of America.

1 2 3 4 5 6 — 00 99 98 97 96 95

FOR PEG BYARS

who is distinguished in commerce
and distinguished in nourishing
new life into new lifestyle among
the many she brings to faith.

CONTENTS

PREFACE

Currently, I live and work in western Canada, where the Christian gospel is not in good shape. The church is weak and disunited, and it has departed widely from its New Testament heritage of faith. There is still a lot of belief in God, there is still substantial nominal attachment to the church, but in practice people live for money and success. The climate of the day is pluralist, the philosophy of the day is hedonist.

And yet the gospel of Jesus Christ still has its ancient power. It is not as if it has been tried and found wanting. It has simply not been tried.

This very morning in our congregation, which did not even exist four years ago, one person who had been a Christian for only a year or so introduced a friend to me—a friend who had been brought to faith by one of my books that I wrote some time ago. This happens regularly at speaking engagements, I find. People will come up afterward and thank me for introducing them to Christ, who has become the greatest influence in their lives. I will look at them in amazement, never having seen them before, until I realize they are referring to a book I have written that, in the mercy of God, has been of special value to them.

That is why I am glad to revise and reissue this book, written originally twenty years ago. It is not out of date, though some of the illustrations and language were—hence the revision. And it remains relevant precisely because the situation it addresses is every bit as pressing today as it was then. It is all about how to grow and develop in the Christian life after taking those first tentative steps of faith to Jesus Christ. I do not *think* this is a continuing problem. *I know it is!* Wherever I go, I find Christians who lack assurance that they are really in God's family, Christians who are hopelessly defeated, Christians who have no devotional life, Christians who are painfully ignorant even of the basics of discipleship. And so whether it is in post-Christian Canada or among the surging tides of new believers in Tanzania, there is a continuing need for a book that explains in a simple, readable way how to go on with Christ once you have begun with Him.

This is such a book. It is not comprehensive or even adequate. It is not scholarly or hard to follow. It is a book about the basics of Christian living, where I have tried to paint on a broad canvas the main features of the landscape that unfolds before the new believer—or the longtime church member who suddenly stumbles into the recognition of what it is all about. It is meant to help such people to "grow in grace and in the knowledge of our Lord and Savior, Jesus Christ."

I am grateful for the permissions granted me to quote copyrighted material. I have also found it helpful to quote, anonymously, from my correspondence, much of it from new Christians. Thanks are due to Carolyn Armitage and James Catford, both editors at Hodder, for giving a great deal of help in the revision of this book. I am grateful to Edward England, Pat Dearnley, and Roy Catchpole for assistance earlier along the line.

Michael Green
Regent College, Vancouver

ACKNOWLEDGMENTS

I am grateful to the Right Reverend Hugh Montefiore for permission to quote his version of the Ten Commandments, and the Right Reverend Trevor Huddleston for permission to quote from a BBC broadcast. "The Act of Love" by Roger McGough is reprinted from *Love, Love, Love*, edited by Peter Roche, published by Corgi Books Ltd.

BEGINNING
your new life
IN CHRIST

1

TWICE IS THE ONLY WAY TO LIVE!

THE FOURTH DIMENSION

He was a young man in his twenties, hooked on alcohol and drugs. One night, when he was drunk with liquor and high on LSD, he heard about Jesus, the real living Jesus who could take him and change him. He surrendered his life to Christ, and the change began to take place. I met him ten months after this new beginning. He was radiantly happy, self-possessed, and integrated. I asked him how long he had been a Christian. He told me, "Ten months." I asked him if he had introduced any others to Christ in this time, and he laughed—so did the others who were standing around in the room in Toronto where this conversation was taking place. "More than I can remember," was his memorable reply.

I think of an occasion when I was teaching in a theological college. One of our students came to tell me that the previous weekend he had been revisiting a country church where a team from the college had recently conducted a mission. One of his many encouragements was to sit at the back of a room where about thirty villagers of different ages, backgrounds, and outlooks were engaged in a Bible study led by a man and his wife who had found faith in Christ during the mission a couple of months earlier.

It reminded me, as he spoke, of an RAF officer who had become a believer in Christ through reading a book I had written. He gave copies to five couples among his service friends, and then invited them to meet my wife and me in his home one evening. He sat us down, put us at our ease, and then explained why he had invited everyone. He had been a believer only a few weeks himself, and had certainly never heard anyone speak about Jesus Christ to a group of friends in a home. He told us that he would not have believed it if people had informed him two months ago that he would be sitting at a group like that, discussing Jesus. If they had gone on to suggest that *he* might be organizing the group, he would have thought them mad! But he had found Jesus Christ in the meantime—the living Jesus who had begun to make a new man of him. So naturally he wanted to share the news with his friends.

You can imagine how well that evening went. His friends had expected me to talk about Christ—after all, I was a minister and was paid to do that sort of thing. But they hadn't expected anything so definite, so full of a sense of discovery, from *him*. He was like the man in Jesus' parable, who had been plowing a dull and dusty furrow in a field and then suddenly struck a box; on examination, it turned out to be full of treasure. That's what it is like, according to Jesus, when someone discovers the kingdom of God. It's like finding treasure when you weren't expecting anything of the sort. Well, my friend had found treasure, and it made a great impression on his circle.

These people I have mentioned (and the list could be extended indefinitely) have one thing in common. They have found a new world of experience, a new dimension to living. It's as if they have been living in a pond all their lives up till now, like the tadpole. And now they have turned into frogs and have emerged from the pond to start a fresh existence on dry land. Of course, like the frog, they are thoroughly at home in the pool still; they retain all the experiences they had before. But they have this new world opening up to them. It is almost as if they had been born all over again. That was, in fact, how Jesus described it to a learned theologian, who knew all about God and the Scriptures but had never found the treasure of this new life for himself.

NEW LIFE

I am writing this book for people who have begun to emerge from the pool; for those who are making their first cries as infants in the family of God; for those whose eyes have been opened to a new world around them after Jesus has laid His hand on them. I hope I am writing for you. I trust that you know what this new life in Christ means. If you do, you can skip the rest of this chapter. But if you don't, the next bit is rather crucial. Without it the rest of the book won't make any kind of sense. Lots of books on Christian behavior make the cardinal error of assuming you can lay down a code of conduct to be followed and call it Christian ethics *without changing human nature*. I tell you it can't be done.

Incidentally, this is why we all feel that talk about morality is so dull and unattractive. It sets before us a standard that we can't keep; and that is depressing. It presents us with a set of rules; and that makes our hackles rise. We say, "Why should I bother with that one? Why should I keep this?" I have only to see a notice—"Keep Off the Grass"—and I immediately want to trample all over it. Don't you? Very well, we understand each other, you and I. We know that dead orthodoxy, codes of rules, moral behavior patterns leave us cold.

To commend Christian ethics to people who have no Christian faith is to ask for failure if they try to keep the standards and for hypocrisy if they don't. It is as ludicrous as going around tying apples onto a dead apple tree. The only way you will get any satisfaction with apples is to pick them off a live tree. You need to have Christ's new life coursing through your personality before you can produce the fruit of a Christlike character. Obvious enough,

when you come to think of it. You can't have the
new lifestyle without the new life.

DEAD AND ALIVE

Fair enough. But how do you get the new life? The
answer is not difficult. But it is costly. Costly to God,
and costly to us. It is like this. God made men and
women as the crown of His creation. We share in and
transcend the different levels of life displayed in the
rest of creation. A stone has life of a sort; it exists. A
flower has a more developed life, with its ability to
breathe and to feed, to bud, to blossom, and to die
away before the cycle begins again. Animals have a
higher form of life, equipped as they are in varying
degrees with mobility, intelligence, adaptability, and
strength. Some of the monkey family are almost
human in their abilities. But there are very distinct
differences between us and the animals. We can think.
We can pray. We can communicate logically. We can
make ourselves the object of our own reflection. We
have a sense of beauty, of truth, of goodness. We
have a conscience. In all these ways, and others,
we transcend the animal creation. Our lives are fuller
than theirs. We rejoice in our physical, mental, and
aesthetic vitality. Especially if all of these are in good
health, it is just wonderful to be alive.

But the Bible teaches, and experience confirms,
that in a very real sense we are dead while we live.
Dr. Herbert Kohn once wrote in a Sunday newspa-

per: "The biggest single problem facing us is no meaning and purpose. Why do we stay alive? What are we here for? My grandfather walked with God, and knew why—but we don't." That puts the human situation in a nutshell. In the graphic picture given us in the book of Genesis, the human race was made to enjoy God's company—no less. We were meant to "walk with Him in the garden in the cool of the day." We were meant to enjoy this supreme dimension of life—sharing the very company of God who gave us life.

Notice the accent is on sharing. But what did we do? We decided to go it alone. We ate the fruit of the one tree that God had forbidden. And disobedience broke the relationship. We ceased to walk with God. God was no longer a companion to be enjoyed but a sinister figure to be dreaded. He might inquire, "Why are you hiding?" Feeling guilty, we preferred to keep out of God's way. Reluctantly, God endorsed our choice. We human beings were expelled from His garden, cut off from what is picturesquely and significantly described as the tree of life (Gen. 3:24).

We are aliens from our homeland. It has been well said, "Modern man is no longer merely an exile. He has forgotten his home and has no hope of a promised land."

We have rejected this highest range of life, sharing in the fellowship of our Creator. Spiritually speaking, we are already dead. So dead that we are for the most part unaware of God's existence. So dead that we will not listen to His claims on our lives. So dead that any talk about God seems utterly foreign to us, almost as if it were spoken in another language. Jean-Paul Sartre went so far as to claim, "God is dead, even in the hearts of believers." Indeed, many sensitive people feel themselves to be dead. Fellini, the film producer, and director of *La Dolce Vita*, wrote,

> Like many people I have no religion and I am just sitting in a small boat, drifting with the tide. I just go on working, shooting, cutting, editing, looking at life and trying to make others see. Today we stand naked, defenseless and more alone than at any time in history. We are waiting for something—perhaps another miracle, perhaps the Martians—who knows?

True enough! We are indeed waiting for someone to restore meaning and purpose of life. But the man of tomorrow came yesterday. Jesus was His name. That word *Jesus* means, quite literally, "God to the rescue." Christians believe that Jesus was—and is—just that. I don't propose to argue the case for that stupendous claim. I have had a go at it in *World on the Run* and *You Must Be Joking!* But I believe it with all my heart. I have scrutinized the evidence, and I am satisfied. So confident that I am prepared to gamble my future and my life on its truth. And I believe that the whole objective in God becoming one of us for thirty years or so in the first century was to enable us to recover this "high-octane" life, this possibility of life shared with Him, which was lost by human disobedience in the mists of long ago, and which people continue to jettison daily as carelessly as they throw away a plastic cup.

LIFE THROUGH DEATH

How was the situation of broken relationships to be restored so that once again we could enjoy His life? Well, the essence of the operation was this. Jesus came, not primarily to teach us how to live, to heal sick people, or to be an anti-establishment leader, but to bring new life to the spiritually dead. "My purpose is to give life in all its fullness," said Jesus (John 10:10 TLB). Paul, reflecting on Christ's achievement, has this to say, "Time was when you were dead in your sins. In our natural condition we, along with all the rest, lay under the dreadful judgment of God. But God, rich in mercy, for the great love he bore us, brought us to life with Christ, even when we were dead in our sins" (Eph. 2:1–2). The whole New Testament bears witness to the fact that it was through the Cross and resurrection of Jesus that this new life has become available. We *can* live twice!

It is very difficult to understand how Jesus' death so long ago can be of any use to us today, and how it can make any difference to our relationship with God. There are various pictures sketched by the New Testament writers to help us understand. Sometimes they talk as if we were all captives in a foreign land to a hostile power, and the death of

Jesus was the price paid to repatriate us and deliver us from this enemy power. But pursue that analogy too far and you get into trouble. You start asking to whom was the ransom paid, and at once you are in difficulties. So the wise thing to do is to look at another word picture and regain perspective. Sometimes Paul speaks of Jesus dying on the cross as the means of reconciling two estranged parties, us and God. Sometimes he speaks of Jesus as the mediator in a broken relationship (we have plenty of this sort of thing in industrial relations) and He succeeded in restoring good relations only at the cost of His own life. Sometimes New Testament writers see His innocent suffering as the ultimate way in which evil is conquered; once you retaliate, you only double the evil. Jesus not only taught but demonstrated the tremendous moral power of the innocent willingly and lovingly accepting cruelty and brutality at the hands of the guilty in order to absorb and neutralize the wickedness and bring people to their senses.

THE MEANING OF THE CROSS

All of these insights given us by the biblical writers shed some light on His death. But perhaps the simplest and at the same time the most profound way of looking at it is this: *our lives were forfeit; He forfeited His life for us.* That needs spelling out a bit. Our rebellion against God had cut us off from enjoying His company; we were "aliens, without God in the world" (Eph. 2:12). Jesus, on the other hand, Himself both God and man, Himself tempted more strongly than any of us, nevertheless lived a life of perfect obedience. There was no rebellion against God in that life. Rather, He could say with integrity, "I always do those things which please him" (John 8:29).

He had no need to die, physically or spiritually. But die He did, by His own free and deliberate choice. He died physically in great agony on the cross, and spiritually in greater agony as He willingly made Himself responsible for all the horrors, all the filth and guilt of the world's rebellion, including yours and mine. He took your death so that you could have His life. He died in the place where the rebel should have ended up so that the rebel could be adopted into the family from which he had played truant. He died that we might live, forgiven, accepted, in touch with God.

Listen to the thrill of it coming over in Paul's writing. He never got over the wonder of it: "The Son of God loved me, and gave himself for me" (Gal. 2:20). Or again, "We beg you, as though Christ himself were here pleading with you, receive the love he offers you—be reconciled to God. For God took the sinless Christ and poured into him our sins. Then, in exchange, he poured God's goodness into us!" (2 Cor. 5:20–21 TLB).

That idea of the exchange, His life willingly given for our lives that were forfeit, gripped the early Christians and made them deeply indebted to the love of the Lord. I think it explains why they gave so much notice to Barabbas in the story of the crucifixion. The cross on which Jesus died was meant for Barabbas. He deserved it, if anyone did. He was a robber, an insurgent, and a murderer. Yes, he deserved to die. His life was justly forfeit. But Jesus took his place. He died on Barabbas's cross, though He didn't deserve to. And Barabbas went free because Jesus died on his cross, though he didn't deserve to, either. That exchange seemed to get to the heart of the meaning of the Cross for the first disciples—our lives through His death.

Just after the New Testament period an unknown Christian wrote in these terms about what the Cross meant to him:

> He himself took on him the burden of our iniquities, the holy one for sinners, the immortal for mortals. For what else could cover our sins but his righteousness? O sweet exchange! O work of God beyond all searching out! That the wickedness of many should be hidden by a single righteous one, and that the righteousness of one should put many transgressors right with God. (*Epistle to Diognetus*, 9)

ANY QUESTIONS?

A few quick questions come to mind at this point. "Surely it is not fair of God to punish Christ for our misdeeds?" That is not what the New Testament says. It is not as though God was determined to take it out on somebody for the broken relationship, and if we were to get off scot-free, then He would make Christ pay. That is a travesty of the truth. No, we read, "God was in Christ, reconciling the world to himself" (2 Cor. 5:19). No third party was involved. God, in Christ, personally undertook to restore human relations with Himself, though it involved nothing short of death and hell for Him.

But again, people often ask me, "How can the death of Christ so long ago possibly be effective for sins that hadn't even been committed then—mine, for instance?" Part of the answer to this is to realize that the Cross gives us a window into God's unchanging attitude toward human rebellion. He always has to judge it, and He always determines to taste its ashes Himself so as to deliver us from the results of our willfulness and folly (if we will allow Him to). And part of the answer lies in the fact that Christ laid down His infinite life on that cross for the finite number of people in the world, and the finite, large though it be, is always outweighed by the infinite. On the cross we see God dealing in person, dealing at unspeakable cost, with the problem of human rebellion at its very root. Because He was going to do so, He could gladly accept anyone who lived B.C. Because He has done so, He can gladly accept anyone who lives A.D. The Cross lies at the midpoint of time and can avail for all.

"But does that mean that this new life you talk of

is free, and that I have nothing to pay?" people ask.
That is precisely what it does mean. Suppose you
are in debt to the tune of thousands of dollars and
are absolutely broke. And suppose your creditor
says, "Right, you can go free. The debt is canceled,
and here's $50,000 to start you off in a new life."
What can you do but take it in wonder and gratitude, and say a heartfelt "Thank you"? To attempt
to pay for it would be as impossible as it would be
impertinent. That, said Jesus, is the position we
must take up before God's offer of a new life. We are
His debtors, and He declares our debts discharged.
We were doomed to death under His laws, and He
tells us, "Your doom is remitted. You are free to live
a new life." You can't pay for something like that.
You can only take a royal pardon *as* a pardon; take it
and be profoundly grateful.

But we have still been considering only half of the
story. If the Cross means that Jesus forfeited His life
for ours, which lay forfeit, the Resurrection means
that His new life can surge into our dead spirits.
This is just what the early Christians found. To their
amazement, they discovered that Jesus was not
dead and gone. He rose from the grave that third
day; the tomb was empty, the last enemy defeated.
Jesus had tried conclusions with death, our greatest
foe, and He had overcome. "It was not possible for
him to be held down by it," they concluded (Acts
2:24). The only person who had lived a life of perfect
obedience, Jesus was the only person on whom
death, the fruit of human rebellion against God,

could maintain no grip. He rose, and He is alive today, thank God. When someone becomes a Christian, it means that this person allows the risen Christ to come into his or her spirit and take up residence. And the Christian life is no less than Christ's own life struggling to show itself from inside us.

It is as if our lives are gardens—derelict, overgrown, and devoid of fruit trees. The day we become Christians, the Holy Spirit is planted in the garden. He has to contend with lots of weeds that always hinder, sometimes threaten to stifle any growth completely. The climate is often cold, and the neglect to which the plant is subjected is something awful. But gradually, over the years, the tender sapling grows into a fruitful tree, and people come and refresh themselves with the luscious fruit, even though there are still plenty of nettles round the base. That is how the new life of Christ takes root in our personalities and makes itself known even though every one of us still has a long way to go.

Paul can rightly say, "The fruit of the Spirit is love, joy, peace, patience, kindness, generosity, faithfulness, gentleness, and self-control (Gal. 5:22–23 NRSV). Those lovely, mature fruits of Christian living are only possible when Christian life has begun, when the Spirit of the risen Christ has been welcomed into your life. Remember, it's no good tying apples onto a dead tree. You achieve nothing and only make yourself look ridiculous. You have to live twice!

FROM DEATH TO LIFE

The issue is now crystal clear. It comes to this. Have you got new life? Has the Holy Spirit been planted in your life? "If anyone does not have the Spirit," said Paul, "he is no Christian" (Rom. 8:9). We may have been born in a Christian country, and have gone to a Christian school at the instigation of fond Christian parents. We may have attended church regularly and be able to say the creed backward! But if we have not made room for the Holy Spirit to come into our lives, whatever else we are, we are not yet Christians. It sounds hard, but it isn't really. Plants can't bear fruit until they have been planted and taken root. People can't grow and develop until they have been born. Obvious, isn't it? And yet so many people fail to see it when it comes to spiritual things. You can't live the Christian life until you have been born into the Christian family. You can't produce Christian character until the Holy Spirit has been planted in your life.

Has He? You know if this has happened or not. You and God. If you know you have not begun, I suggest that before you go any farther in this book, you get this matter sorted out once and for all with God. It doesn't matter how you express yourself. It's your attitude of giving in to God that matters. If it helps, you could say something like this:

God, I begin to see why You have seemed so unreal to me. I have been alive physically and mentally, but spiritually dead all these years, cut off from Your life. No wonder I was very doubtful at times whether You even existed. But I do thank You very much for coming to meet me in my confusion. Thank You for Jesus and His amazing love in being willing to go to that cross for me. I don't understand it all, but I believe He did it for me, and that because He died there, I can be forgiven and have the past wiped out. That is a wonderful welcome, God, and I don't deserve it. I can't begin to earn it. So I won't try. I shall simply come to You and say "Thank You." And I am putting the rest of my life at Your disposal. I want to use it for You now. I want the life of the risen Christ to come in and possess me. I want Him to shine out through me. God, You have shown me through the cross of Jesus that You accept me, just as I am. Well, here and now I accept You. You're going to have to look after me, Lord, because I know I can't make it on my own. But then, I don't have to, do I? For You have promised that You will come and share Your very own life with me. Please come in, Lord, and do just that.

You know, that old James Bond film was quite right, more right than its producers realized: "You only live twice . . . and twice is the only way to live."

2

GETTING IT STRAIGHT

TWO TYPES OF FEELINGS

Once you put your hand in the hand of Christ, a new life begins. To quote Paul again, "When someone becomes a Christian he becomes a brand new person inside. He is not the same any more. A new life has begun!" (2 Cor. 5:17 TLB). Sometimes the new life bursts exuberantly on the scene.

This, for instance, is how one person wrote to me recently, five days after surrendering her life to Christ. She was a mature person, a mother, a strong character, and an experienced hostess. She was certainly not the emotional sort. Would you understand what I mean if I tell you she was a general's widow? Well, this is what she wrote:

> I must write and tell you what a tremendous experience this has been for me. No words can explain it. If anyone had told me last week that I should feel like I do this week, I am afraid I would not have believed it. In the past I have not prayed very much, or gone to church very much,

and still I seldom read the Bible. I want you to know that it was for this reason that I wavered so long on Saturday morning, taking so much of your time. I did not think I could be ready to take such a step. But how right you were, and my heart is full of thankfulness: to Graham for bringing me to you, to you for bringing me to Christ, and to Christ, above all, for entering in, for there is absolutely no doubt about it. In fact I still feel rather in the clouds, but I know that there is a lot of work to be done as soon as I return home.

Yes, some people feel like that immediately when they start the new life. But some people don't. Here is another reaction after almost exactly the same period of a few days:

Really, I scarcely know what has happened to me this week. Perhaps this is the best test of the validity that God really did respond and come into my heart—that there was no spectacular emotional experience, of which I would have been very mistrustful; but somehow there really was something different. I felt as if I was being pushed from one thing to another all through the usual routine, by something inside me. Instead of frantically trying to plan my time to fit everything in, I scarcely had to think about it. I'm still afraid that the assurance will not last. I didn't really believe that I could have a personal relationship like this with God, so I suppose it is natural for me to be surprised and rather unsure of it. It's too soon to say, "It has made such and such a difference in my life." At present I want to get to know him better.

That last sentence could almost be the theme of this book. It is the authentic Christian longing. Having found Christ, we want to explore Him more and more, and to give ourselves over to Him in every department of our lives. That is the very heart of the Christian life: getting to know Him better, and working out the implications of it in our behavior and attitudes, our careers and relationships.

We shall be examining some of these areas in subsequent chapters. But there is a prior issue to sort out. It came up in both of those quotations from my correspondents. It is the problem of what to do with our doubts and how far we should allow our Christian assurance to be governed by our feelings.

DEALING WITH DOUBTS

There are a good many uncertainties and doubts we cannot avoid; and in our own generation these are far more pressing than ever before. Insecurity arising from the threat of unemployment, poverty, political and industrial unrest, broken relationships, and the general state of the world today. These are uncertainties we have to live with. However, we can have, and are meant to have, complete confidence that we belong to Christ. Indeed, unless we are sure about this relationship with Him, we shall be able neither to develop it nor to introduce others to Him. We would be building the house of our lives on sand instead of rock.

But doesn't any suggestion that Christians can be sure where they stand smack of smugness and self-confidence? That is an accusation often made, but it is simply not the case. Of course, there are Christians who are smug, but that is their fault, not the fault of their Christianity. It is possible to be sure without being smug.

Suppose you give your child a bicycle for Christmas. You mean for her to know that she has it, don't you? She can be sure of your gift, but she has nothing to crow about. She didn't earn it: it's a gift.

Now it is like that with God. If we start thinking about what we deserve, the New Testament tells us straight: "The wages of sin is death." We do not and cannot earn new life. "The *free gift* of God is eternal life through Jesus Christ our Lord" (Rom. 6:23 TLB). New life is His gift: I know I've got it, but I also know it is entirely due to His generosity, not to my merits. That is what the famous phrase "justification by faith" means. We are justified, acquitted, put right with God (a status that nothing can destroy) not by our "works," our efforts at self-justification, but by "grace," God's undeserved favor to us (Eph. 2:8–9; Rom. 3:24–25). And this we receive by "faith," by trusting Him.

So now, since we have been justified by faith, we can have real peace with God because of what Jesus Christ our Lord has done for us. In response to our faith, he has brought us to this place of highest privilege in which we stand, and we rejoice in the expectation of becoming all that God has in mind for us to be (Rom. 5:1–2).

Is It Wrong to Be Sure?

What I want to ask those Christians who believe it is wrong to be sure about their relationship with Christ is this: "Do you know what family you belong to? Do you know if you're married?" Of course they know and would never dream of saying, "Well, I *think* I am in the Green family and that my name is Michael, but I'm really not sure," or "I think I'm married; I hope I'm married, but it is presumptuous to say that I *am* married." What nonsense that would be. It is just as nonsensical and much more impertinent to doubt God. He says that we are the bride, and Christ is the bridegroom; we are linked to Him forever in the closest of all possible ties. He says that He adopts us into His family so that we are children in the family of God and fellow heirs with Christ of all His bounty (2 Cor. 11:2; Rom. 8:15–17). He says it, He means it, and we can take Him at His word.

It comes down to this, really: trust. As in all personal relationships, trust is fundamental. How does the wife know her husband won't be unfaithful to her? How does the patient know the doctor won't poison him? How does the client know the lawyer won't swindle him? How does the child know that her mother loves her? The answer in each case is simply trust. Why should it be different with God?

Christ says He will accept you: "The one who comes to me I will never, no never, throw out" (John 6:37). And you have come to Him as best you know how. Very well then, He *has* accepted you, for the simple and utterly sufficient reason that He said He would. Your feelings may be up or down: it matters not one whit. Your experience is nil to start with. You have nothing but His naked word to go on. But it is enough. It brought assurance to Dr. Livingstone over a century ago as he struggled with doubt and loneliness in the jungles of central Africa. He recorded in his journal his reflections on the promise of Jesus I have just quoted. And his comment was, "That is the word of a gentleman of the most strict and sacred honour. He cannot break his word." A very Victorian way of putting it, but the point is unarguable.

Very well. We have God's word of acceptance. The God you cannot see offers to accept you into His family when there is nothing you can do to deserve it—and a great deal to disqualify you. What are you to do with such an offer? You trust His word, for a start. And then you discover, to your amazement, that God gives you a remarkable adoption certificate—baptism.

The Mark of Belonging

Baptism is the mark of Christian belonging. Christians in the Baptist tradition believe this should be by total immersion and only after you have put your faith in Christ. Most other Christian churches believe that it is immaterial whether baptism precedes faith or faith precedes baptism, so long as you believe in your heart and have this outward mark of baptism upon you. But both traditions are clear about its importance.

You only have to go to a predominantly Muslim or Buddhist country to discover how baptism sets you apart. You may believe secretly, and nobody worries too much. But as soon as you get baptized, then you have to face the music. I remember several of my Jewish friends of student days being disowned by their parents because they had confessed Christ, not merely in personal faith but in open baptism. Baptism is, therefore, very much the mark of discipleship: the irrevocable pledge that I belong to Christ and am committed to being "His faithful soldier and servant until my life's end."

It is important to stress the decisiveness of Christian baptism as the mark to others that I am a follower of Christ. It is even more important to stress the decisiveness of Christian baptism as the mark God gives to me to assure me that I belong. If, in a moment of doubt, a young bride separated from her husband finds herself wondering whether she is really married or whether it is all just a dream, she only has to glance down at her ring. There it is, the mark of belonging, the love gift from her bridegroom to assure her that she does belong to him for keeps.

Baptism acts as a physical reassurance of our relationship with Christ. He accepts us, forgives us, adopts us into His family, and offers us His Holy

Spirit to live in us, not because we have done a thing to deserve it but simply because God is love. In His love He came to this world for us. In His love He died for us. In His love He welcomes us, irrespective of our qualifications. And baptism graphically declares this.

To Assure You

The important thing is that all Christians should be baptized. If you have committed your life to Christ and have not yet been baptized, you are clearly bidden by the New Testament to get baptized. Baptism and belief belong together as the visible and the invisible sides of the same relationship. If you have already been baptized as an infant and have subsequently come to faith, there is no indication in the Bible that you should be rebaptized—rather the reverse. Baptism is the sacrament of justification, of the new birth, of becoming a Christian, of receiving the Spirit, of entering God's family (Rom. 6:3–4; Gal. 3:26–27). The new beginning happens only once; logically, then, the sacrament of initiation cannot be repeated.

But the point I want to stress is this. Whether you were baptized as an infant or a grown-up, your baptism is the mark of your faith and of God's gracious acceptance of you. Seen in this light, it is a visible, tangible promise. It is as if God says to you by it, "Yes, I know you have let Me down since you came to faith. I know you are racked with doubts. But I have given you this mark of baptism in your body to assure you that you are accepted, unacceptable as you may be in yourself. You are now in the family, through My dear Son, Jesus Christ."

As time goes on, you won't be tempted to doubt in the same way as you are tested initially. There's no point. The devil realizes it is a loss to tempt an older, experienced Christian with doubts about whether he has really begun the Christian life or not. I may have thought it incredible that Rosemary, my wife, should care about me in the earliest days of our love, but now we've been happily married for years and doubts of her love never cross my mind. We have had too much experience of living together to doubt its reality and the strength of our relationship. And it is like that with the Christian. As the months and years go by, you will discover that the devil finds plenty of other ways of tripping you up, but leaves this initial gambit pretty much alone. You will also discover that you have become as sure of your relationship with Christ as you are with some friend you know and love well.

A LETTER FOR DOUBTERS

One of the New Testament letters was written for people who had not so long ago entrusted their lives to Jesus Christ. John tells us at the end of his gospel that its supreme purpose was to bring people to the conviction that Jesus was God's Son and, further, to that personal encounter with Jesus that would start them off on a new life. He wrote his first letter, he tells us, to people who already believe in Jesus so that "they may know that they have eternal life" (1 John 5:13)—this new quality of existence of which we spoke in chapter 1. Notice that word *know*. We are meant to be in no doubt about it. And in that letter John outlines several of the ways in which the new life will make itself felt.

New Sense of Pardon

There's a new sense of forgiveness. Those who cannot even forgive themselves are assured, as they look at the Cross, that they are forgiven by God:

If you sin, there is someone to plead for you before the Father. His name is Jesus Christ, the one who is all that is good and who pleases God completely. He is the one who took God's wrath against our sins upon himself, and brought us into fellowship with God; and he is the forgiveness for our sins, and not only ours but all the world's (1 John 2:1–2 TLB).

New Desire to Please God

Then there's a new desire to go God's way. Previously, I did not care too much if I did wrong, so long as I was not found out. But now I do begin to care—even if nobody is watching. Because I know that wrongdoing was the thing that took my Lord to the cross. It hurts Him. And I don't want to hurt the One I have begun to love:

> Someone may say, "I am a Christian; I am on my way to heaven; I belong to Christ." But if he doesn't do what Christ tells him to, he is a liar. . . . That is the way to know whether or not you are a Christian. Anyone who says he is a Christian should live as Christ did (1 John 2:4–6 TLB).

New Attitude to Others

A third pointer is a new attitude to other people: "So now we can tell who is a child of God and who belongs to Satan. Whoever is living a life of sin and doesn't love his brother shows that he is not in God's family" (1 John 3:10 TLB). In other words, we see the man next door not just as a nasty piece of work (which he may very well be—but then so are we, until Jesus gets to work on us). We see him as the nasty piece of work for whom Christ was content to die. And if Jesus did that for him, well, it rather changes things, does it not? We begin to see others as Christ sees them and to act accordingly.

New Care for Christians

There's a very special side to this new love that characterizes Christians. It is a love for other believers, a sense of belonging to them in the same family. Indeed, so significant is this that John gives it as one of the ways of deciding whether a person is a Christian or not: "If we love other Christians it proves that we have been delivered from hell and given eternal life. . . . We know what real love is from Christ's laying down his life for us. And so we ought to lay down our lives for our Christian brothers" (1 John 3:14–16 TLB). That is just what the early Christians did, and it so impressed the world that people exclaimed, "See how these Christians love one another." Sadly, in many churches today there is little of that infectious merriment and unselfish love for other Christians; instead, you find rather a carping and critical spirit. But that is not the true family characteristic.

I have had the chance in recent years of going into many parts of the world—Africa, the Far East, Australia, and North America—and I have been more than ever struck by this love for fellow Christians that always springs from true conversion. You may never have seen them before; you may never see them again. But even in a short meeting you seem to go right down to bedrock with other members of the Jesus family. You feel that you have known them for years. You sense that you are on the same wavelength, forgiven sinners, people with a message and a new purpose in life, with the same Holy Spirit at work changing you from inside. This love for other Christians, irrespective of color, background, or nationality (Col. 3:11–12), is one of the most precious gifts God gives His children—and thereby assures us that we really do belong.

New Power Over Evil

Do you want another sign of the new life surging within? Here it is: "The person who has been born into God's family does not make a practice of sinning, because God's new life is in him; so he can't keep on sinning, for this new life has been born in him and controls him—he has been *born again*" (1 John 3:9 TLB). In other words, there is a new power released within Christians, none other than Christ Himself who is now resident inside us. Of course, Christians can and do sin. John knows that perfectly well (1 John 1:8–9). What is more, he knows the way of pardon for the guilty Christian conscience—as we come straight back to our heavenly Father, tell Him the mess we made, and rely on His forgiveness, which is guaranteed to us by the cross of Jesus. But sin should increasingly become the exception, not the rule. The new life in us does not do what is wrong because it is God's life at work in us. Insofar as we allow that new life free play, we shall find that the power of Christ does deliver us daily from the forces of evil that have for so long dragged us down.

It is interesting that the first letter I had from a newly converted Canadian friend, whose life had been in a bad way, made this very point about a new power let loose in him: "I purposely have not written to you until now, because I wanted to see if what had happened to me would last," he wrote after a couple of months. "It has lasted! . . . My craving for alcohol and cigarettes left me immediately, and I have had no desire for either of them since." How about that? The power of alcoholism and the power of smoking were snapped overnight, as if the Lord was giving him a foretaste of what He could do. Of course he had a long way to go. There were plenty of battles to come, and he may have had a sense of what was to come when writing what followed: "My resentments are gone, and my fears, but I find that when I'm not watching they can sometimes creep up on me again." Don't we all? What is the way to meet them then? My friend had already discovered it: "So I have to keep on coming back to God. But the big difference is that now I have him to come back to." The Christian life begins with Christ and continues with Christ. He is the only One who can change us. And the wonder of it is that He does, if we let Him, and just as much as we let Him. It is perfectly true that "every child of God can obey him, defeating sin and evil pleasure by trusting Christ to help him" (1 John 5:4 TLB).

New Joy and Confidence

There are other things that gradually emerge as we press further and further into the new country of life with Christ. For one thing, there is the joy He gives. John says that he wrote this letter "so that you, too, may be full of joy," a joy that comes from "our fellowship with the Father and his Son Jesus Christ" (1 John 1:3–4). For another thing, there is the still, gentle voice of the Holy Spirit inside us, assuring us that we are in the family. "The man who believes in the Son has this voice of testimony within him," says John, "the voice of the Holy Spirit in our hearts" (1 John 5:10).

It is not easy to describe what this means to anyone who has not experienced it, any more than it is to describe what it means to be loved to someone who has had a loveless life. John does make an attempt in another place in his letter:

> We know how much God loves us because we have felt his love and because we believe him when he tells us that he loves us dearly. God is love, and anyone who lives in love is living with God and God is living in him. And as we live with Christ, our love grows more perfect and complete; so we will not be ashamed and embarrassed at the day of judgment, but can face him with confidence and joy, because he loves us and we love him too (1 John 4:16–17 TLB).

If you've been a Christian even for a short time, you'll understand what John is talking about. That is what is meant by the inner witness of the Holy Spirit.

New Experience of Prayer

One other thing begins to change: prayer. I shall have more to say about that in the next chapter, but just for the moment notice this. John marvels at the new experience of answered prayer that opens up once we come into the family of God. In the old days, nobody seemed to be there; nobody seemed to listen. Prayer was a hopeless exercise; it did no good; and probably we gave it up entirely, except perhaps as a last resort in some emergency.

Look at the change now: "We are confident of this, that he will listen to us whenever we ask him for anything in line with his will. And if we really know he is listening when we talk to him and make our requests, then we can be sure that he will answer us" (1 John 5:14–15). A new world, you see. No longer is God a stranger, but a friend, a father, one who delights to have us talk to Him and open up the whole of our lives to Him. And no less amazing, we begin to want to do it. We actually come to enjoy prayer. Fantastic, but true, as any Christian will tell you. It is one of the signs of new life.

So these are some of the marks of God's new vitality, which gradually makes itself felt in different aspects of our lives. They take time. But they do come. They justify Paul's tremendous claim with which we began, that "when someone becomes a Christian he becomes a brand new person inside. He is not the same any more. A new life has begun!" (2 Cor. 5:17 TLB).

A Fresh Perspective

He was writing to me to describe the change in attitude that had come about since he became a Christian:

> It is rather like a cyclist who, when he has climbed a long hill, feels he should be able to freewheel down the other side. It is not until he reaches the top that he sees that his task has only just started, and that the road winds on, with even steeper hills than the one he has just climbed. When people accept Christ, they tend to think it will all be freewheeling from that point. But then they discover it is only the beginning. At least, that's the case in my experience.

And in mine, too. Now why should this be?

It is important to get clear about this right away because it is bound to influence the way we approach the rest of our Christian life. Why is it harder once you have become a Christian than it ever was before?

GOING WITH THE CROWD

It is harder because in the old days you were largely influenced by what *you* wanted to do, by the group you went around with, or by what happened to be the fashion or the good cause of the moment. On the whole you saw no particular reason to be different, unless it suited you to be. You went with the crowd. It was more convenient that way. Anyhow, what could one individual do, even if you wanted to? So why bother? According to most people, right and wrong are just matters of personal choice or convention. They don't hold good for all people everywhere. So why not take the easy way, the way that pays best? After all, the world isn't going anywhere. There is nothing that ultimately matters. We came from nothing and we go to nothing. So make the best of it.

Get as wide a range of experience out of life as you can. That's what it's there for. If you should die young, it would be a pity to have missed any of it. So by all means take crack and sleep with anyone you like, provided nobody gets too badly hurt. It will be interesting to find out what each new experience is like. And why not? There is no heaven or hell, no God or devil—or *is* there a devil, after all? There's certainly something in all this Satan wor-

ship and black magic. But anyhow, there is no God
we can be sure about. So nothing is forbidden
unless, of course, you personally don't like it. Do
your own thing and enjoy it. I'll do mine.

These are among the current attitudes of modern
people, especially the young. And they are very reasonable, too: reasonable, that is, if you don't believe
in a God of truth. Today a generation has arisen that
doesn't so much reject the idea that God exists but is
willing uncritically to accept any god, or gods. The
current rise of the New Age beliefs is proof of this.
They claim that as in the physical world anything is
possible, so in the spiritual world anything is
acceptable. Do your own thing. Everything is per-
mitted.

Let's have a closer look at this notion. What I am
saying is this. People today have knocked the
Absolute out of their world and are left with only
the relative. There is no absolute standard for
human behavior left—so we can set up our own
standards of what is acceptable. There is no absolute
standard for truth left, and so even the philosophers
have given up trying to discover the nature of truth,
justice, and goodness that they used to wrestle with.
Instead, they have taken to analyzing words. And
in a society increasingly influenced by New Age ideology, rationality is commonly subordinated to
feeling. "Is it true?" gives place to "Is it relevant?"
Much new legislation is based not on principle but
on attempting to determine what most people want.
In industry or in personal relationships, the notion

of "I want" is paramount; "I ought" is at a discount.
It is the terrible but logical outworking of pluralism.

SWIMMING AGAINST
THE CURRENT

Now do you see why it is harder to be a
Christian than it was to stay uncommitted? Then
you swam with the current. Now you are up
against it in every conceivable way. You have
dared to put the Absolute back into the picture.
You have recognized God and His truth as the center of all existence, and you have gotten in touch
with Him. You belong to a minority, a guerrilla
band. You are out on your own.

Others may think life has no real meaning or purpose. You know it has. Life is meant to be shared
with the Source of all being.

Others may think that the world is the result of a
fluke or the influence of the stars. You know it is the
product of a wise and loving Creator, not some "god
within you" but the God of heaven and earth.

Others may think that the universe is silent and
unfeeling. You know it shouts aloud of your loving
heavenly Father who made it, and who discloses
Himself in the color and scent of every rose or the
glory of every sunset.

Others may think that human personality is
thrown up by luck in a world that is basically mech-
anistic. You know that it is the highest gift of a per-

sonal God. That's why human beings matter so infinitely. They are made in His likeness.

Others may think that truth and beauty and goodness are merely a matter of taste or a transcendental experience. To you, they are different aspects of the Lord Himself, who is the model of goodness, the source of beauty, and the essence of truth.

Others may see that love is the one hope for humanity but have no answer to the problem of why we should bother to love and how we can manage to do it. For you, love is the personal trademark of the Creator, Himself love, who has shared something of His very nature with us—even with those who don't believe in Him. And as a Christian, you bother because all people are the object of that love of His; you cannot manage to love others by your own efforts. It didn't take you long to discover that. But once allow the love of God to reach you and it's bound to find a way out through you to others.

Everything, yes everything, is different once God is restored to His rightful place. And you have done that, haven't you? He is in the middle of the picture? Then don't be surprised that things are tough. What revolutionary ever had them easy? And Christianity is for revolutionary spirits, not for pale conformists. It is for people who have the courage to be different.

A Changed Life—God's Will

I think the greatest area of difference is going to be our behavior. And you will have noticed that this is precisely what people expect. No sooner claim to be a Christian at work than they will expect you not to swear and not to tell dirty stories. They will expect you to clock in on time and work hard. No matter what they may say about not wanting Holy Joes about the place, ordinary nonreligious people expect a Christian to be different and to have higher standards than themselves. And that, though it is rather embarrassing and challenging, is a healthy instinct. I'll tell you why.

Wherever you look in the religions of the world, you will find few essential links between religion and morality, except in the religion of Israel, which flowered in Christianity. You worshiped a god or gods in the pagan religions of the ancient world so as to have an insurance policy in times of trouble and to fulfill the instinct to worship, which is found in every nation under the sun. But your worship did not make many—if any—ethical demands on you, apart, maybe, from a few taboos, such as a ritual bath or abstinence from sexual relations for a few days before worship. Worship and morals were not linked.

But with Israel it was different. It was not a bit of good worshiping the Lord if the worshiper then went out to sell needy people for a pair of shoes. God was not to be kept quiet with a worship service on the weekend while people continued oppressing poor people and swindling their neighbors during the week.

The need for righteous living among those who

claim to worship a righteous God cannot be overemphasized. God, the source of all that is good and true and upright, demands these same qualities in His worshipers. Not, mind you, as a condition of accepting them. We have already seen that He accepts us just as we are. But in due course He does expect the family likeness to become visible in members of His family.

He has gone to considerable trouble to make Himself plain on that point. He does not leave us with mere generalities, evocative though they may be, such as "You must be holy for I am holy, says the Lord" (1 Pet. 1:16). Throughout the Bible, and particularly in the writings of the Old Testament prophets, God lets us know what this holiness of character is going to mean in ordinary, daily behavior. But we aren't very good, on the whole, at listening to other people, even if they are prophets, lecturing us about right and wrong! We are much more liable to be moved by a good example. So that is just what God, in His generosity, provided.

A Changed Life—Jesus' Example

Jesus Christ came not only to be our rescuer from the mess we had gotten ourselves in but to be our example of the right way to live. He lived the perfect life. Never a foot wrong. Never a word out of place. Never a loving act neglected. Never a need unmet. In Jesus Christ we see the ideal for human life. Perfection walked this earth in His person. We no longer need to wonder what the good life might involve. We can no longer plead ignorance. It is there before us, plain for all to see. Unlike any other teacher before or since, Jesus actually lived up to His own teaching. He who told people to love their enemies did that very thing. He who told people not to lay up treasure on earth was so poor that He had no home. He who told people not to worry about their food and clothes lived a life of radiant peace despite the lack of what we would consider even the necessities of life.

Examine the moral teaching of Jesus and I think you'll find that He completely lived up to His own standards. His life was a moral miracle. He showed us not just by His unique teaching but by His matchless living what holiness meant, what the character of God was like. And the implication was painfully obvious. "Christ . . . is your example," cried Peter (and he should know, having lived three years in Jesus' company, watching His every move). *"Follow in his steps!* He never sinned, never told a lie, never answered back when insulted; when he suffered he did not threaten to get even; he left his case in the hands of God who always judges fairly" (1 Pet. 2:21–23 TLB, emphasis added).

But does that really help? It is one thing to recognize that the God we worship is holy and expects us to become increasingly like Him. It is another to realize that He has given us a personal demonstration in terms of a human life to show us what He means by practical holiness. But my trouble is, how can I begin to match up to a standard like that?

A Changed Life—the Spirit's Power

Well, once again, God has made the necessary provision for us. Paul puts it in a nutshell in his first letter to the Christians in Thessalonica, fresh converts from paganism in northern Greece. In almost the same breath he sets before them Christian standards, "God wants you to be holy and pure," and Christian resources, "God gives us his Holy Spirit" (1 Thess. 4:3, 8). The holy God does not lower His standards. He gives us the Holy Spirit to enable us to keep them. When we respond to Jesus, we allow the Holy Spirit to enter our lives. And gradually that Spirit will, as we saw in chapter 1, repel the forces of evil habit from our lives: "So now the fair claims of God's standards can be achieved in us, if we do not live with the self in control but with the Spirit" (Rom. 8:4).

Paul knows what a battlefield his life has become since he declared himself a follower of Jesus: "I love to do God's will so far as my new nature is concerned; but there is something else deep within me, in my lower nature, that is at war with my mind and wins the fight and makes me a slave to the sin that is still within me" (Rom. 7:22–23 TLB). That is the problem. God does not remove the tendency to evil that lies deeply entwined with the very roots of our nature as human beings. But He does give us His

Holy Spirit to combat it. Jesus Christ was always victorious in His battle with evil, facing it as He did continuously through His life, and supremely in the crisis of the Cross. He was the conqueror, all along the line. And the Holy Spirit is given to us, among other things, to work out in us Christ's victory over evil. "Who will free me from my slavery to this deadly lower nature?" cries Paul. "Thank God! It has been done by Jesus Christ our Lord. He has set me free" (Rom. 7:25 TLB).

Yes, He has broken the back of evil. He pioneered the way. He sets us free from condemnation, free from despair, to enable us to fight evil. And we fight (if we are wise) not in our own strength but in His. When tempted, we should look to His Holy Spirit who lives inside us and say, "Lord, please give me Your self-control, Your generosity, Your peace of mind (or whatever it is) *now*." And He will. You will find that, like Paul, you will be able to say, "The power of the life-giving Spirit of Christ has set me free from the vicious circle of sin and death" (Rom. 8:2).

Now let us get two things very clear about this life-changing power of the Spirit. In the first place, the change doesn't happen automatically. In the second place, it doesn't happen overnight.

Change Doesn't Happen Automatically

The Spirit of Jesus isn't going to force change on you. He didn't force His way into your life, did He?

Well, He won't force you to go His way. If you determine to hold on to some evil habit, He will not stop you. It just grieves Him very much. He will reluctantly not be able to use you as fully as He wants. But He is love. And love never forces itself on the beloved. I remember asking a wise Christian in the early days of my Christian life why I could not get power over one particular thing in my life, although I had seen Christ clean up a number of other areas. He asked me, "Did you *want* His power, Michael?" Of course, I had to admit that I did not. I wanted to go my own way. Sadly, the Lord would not stop me. So be very clear about this. Christ can and will deliver you from any evil habit. He can do it at once. *But you have to be willing to let Him!* That's the rub. When you are willing, His power is a reality that nobody can deny.

There is a very interesting example of this in the area of drug addiction. Several years ago, at the Second International Symposium on Drug Abuse, Frank Wilson, one of the six British delegates, listened to the learned papers being read on the virtual impossibility of keeping real hard-liners off drugs once they left the hospital. Then he quietly informed them of the 60 percent success rate sustained over five years in his explicitly Christian rehabilitation unit at Northwick Park. It certainly raised some eyebrows. Much the same reaction followed a few years later when David Wilkerson, of *The Cross and the Switchblade* fame, was able to show a professional body in the U.S.A. that by means of full-blooded conversion to Christ and filling with the Holy Spirit, he had been able to record a success rate among hardened drug users five times that of any secular agency. The point is inescapable. Christ can transform cases that would otherwise be hopeless. His power can change intractable habits in any one of us.

We all know what the expulsive power of a new affection can do: it can make the teenager forget his motorcycle if once the girl of his dreams really crosses his path! Well, once a man has Christ inside him, he can discover a power to set him free from his own worst nature. "I can do everything God asks me to with the help of Christ who gives me the strength and power," claimed Paul (Phil. 4:13 TLB). And you and I can have the same experience.

Change Doesn't Happen Overnight

Second, beware of thinking you will become Christlike overnight. You won't. Some habits will be very reluctant to give way, just as some ice is so thick that it takes a long time to be thawed out by the warmth of the sun. And even though we may experience immediate deliverance from any particular wrong thing that is getting us down, we will then merely be ready for God to show us something else in our lives that needs attention. The process of refining will go on all through our lives. We shall need time if we are to grow like Jesus. It is a slow process, just like growing a good fruit tree.

Have you ever planted a garden? Then you know how impatient you are for the young apple tree and the pear tree you put in to bear fruit. Not a sign of any yet. But there is life, and there is growth, and next year, perhaps. So be patient. Keep in close touch with the holy God who has called you. Study the life and teaching, the behavior and example of Jesus if you want to know how God wishes you to act and react in the pressures of everyday life. And ask the Holy Spirit who lives inside you to take control of your personality and make you progressively more and more like Jesus.

There is a lovely promise in Paul's second letter to the Corinthians, which speaks of the Holy Spirit changing us from one degree of Christ-reflectingness to another as we live in conscious and constant companionship with Him (2 Cor. 3:18). We won't notice it, but others will. It was said of the early disciples that men observing them "were amazed and realized what being with Jesus had done for them" (Acts 4:13 TLB). That is God's strategy. He wants to take men and women who are humble enough to say sorry and come to Him in simple trust; He wants to rehabilitate them and demonstrate in their changed character what He can achieve even in spoiled human lives when once He is given a chance. That is the strategy, and that is the perspective from which to plan your Christian life. People will not believe you have a new life unless they see a new lifestyle. And when they do see it, they'll be ready to listen about the new life—not before.

4

A Transforming Friendship

1. A FRIENDSHIP THAT LASTS

One of the most staggering statements in the Bible is contained in the simple words of Jesus: "I have not called you servants. . . . I have called you friends" (John 15:15). Jesus is prepared to call us friends. Friends, when we have disobeyed Him. Friends, when we have not wanted to know Him. Friends, when we have been rebels. It is an amazing offer.

Pie in the Sky?

When we commit our lives to Christ, we begin a life of friendship with Him that is meant to go on and get richer and deeper until our dying day. And then we shall see Him face-to-face, and it will be wonderful. The One I now know by faith I shall then see. The One I fitfully love I shall be united to forever. "In your presence is fullness of joy, and at your right hand are pleasures forevermore," sang the psalmist (Ps. 16:11), and I believe it. If the first installment of life with Christ here on earth brings such joy and fulfillment, there is every reason to believe Him when He promises that the climax of it all after this life is over will be infinitely satisfying. This means that I can see my life steadily and see it whole as a friendship from now on with Christ, who will stick with me, change me, and in the end receive me into His presence.

Now notice two things about this Christian hope. It is not pie in the sky when you die. The pie, or a great deal of it, is available as we enjoy the Lord's company day by day. It would be infinitely worthwhile even if this life were all there is. But Jesus has said that this life is not all there is, and He has backed up His words with the Resurrection. I'm prepared to take it from Him. He has penetrated beyond the bounds of death. He knows.

Rewards and Punishments?

No, it is not pie in the sky when you die; nor is it a refined form of selfishness to look forward to heaven. I do not love my Lord Jesus because I fear hell (though I believe that without Christ hell is my portion). I do not love Him because I want to go to heaven (I don't if He is not there; endless existence without Him would be exceedingly tedious and unattractive). I love Him because He went to that cross for me, because He patiently waited until I was willing to make room in my crowded life for Him. I love Him because He is so patient with me when I am such a poor follower of His. That is why I love Him. The thought of reward does not play any significant part in my motivation as a Christian. Nevertheless, I believe Him when He says that "there are many homes up there where my Father lives. . . . When everything is ready, then I will come and get you, so that you can always be with me where I am. If this weren't so, I would tell you plainly" (John 14:2 TLB). I believe in heaven, in short, because Jesus taught it, and I trust Him. If He says our friendship is too precious for Him to scrap it at death, that is good enough for me. It is wonderfully generous of Him to be willing to go on sharing His new life with us forever. Yet it's just like Him—His name is love.

Growing Old with Christ

But this chapter is not about heaven and the ultimate enjoyment of His friendship there, though I think we should lift up our eyes from time to time to the future God has promised us. It is a wonderful thing to recall that life is not slipping away from us as our physical powers decay: we are getting nearer the day when we shall enjoy Christ's loving companionship to the fullest. And that has an enriching and broadening effect upon the character. One older Christian man, when asked his age, replied with a smile, "The bright side of seventy." He knew what he was talking about. That is why for the Christian, old age is not an unmitigated menace, nor is death the worst thing that can befall him. As Paul contemplated the process of aging and the approach of death, he wrote,

> We never give up. Though our bodies are dying, our inner strength in the Lord is growing every day. These troubles and sufferings of ours are, after all, quite small and won't last very long. Yet this short time of distress will result in God's richest blessing upon us forever and ever! . . . How weary we grow of our present bodies. That is why we look forward eagerly to the day when we shall have heavenly bodies which we shall put on like new clothes. . . . We look forward with confidence to our heavenly bodies, realizing that every moment we spend in these earthly bodies is time spent away from our eternal home in heaven with Jesus (2 Cor. 4:16–17; 5:2, 6 TLB).

What man could write like that if he did not share the friendship of Christ now and expect its consummation hereafter?

The Supreme Ambition

Yes, Christ is the friend who will receive us at the end of our lives, just as Christ was the friend who accepted us in the first place. The Christian life begins and ends with Him. It is significant that Paul, who came to know Christ initially on the Damascus Road, should disclose, some quarter of a century later, what was his supreme ambition in these words: "My aim is to know him" (Phil. 3:10). *To know Him:* that was the very center of Christian living for the great apostle. He knew Him already, of course. He had known Him over a quarter of a century in times of success and loneliness, elation and depression, in the banqueting hall and in the dungeon, on dry land and in shipwreck, and yet his aim was to know Him better. Perhaps in that simple ambition we have plumbed the innermost secret of the greatness of Paul. Christ was his friend, and for that friend he was willing to work and to suffer, come what may. But most of all, he wanted to know Him better. He would have approved of the famous prayer of Richard of Chichester:

Thanks be to thee, my Lord Jesus Christ,
For all the benefits thou hast won for me,
For all the pains and insults thou hast borne for me.
O most merciful Redeemer, Friend and Brother,
May I know thee more clearly,
Love thee more dearly,
And follow thee more nearly
For thy name's sake.

2. A FRIENDSHIP THAT DEVELOPS

The Phone and the Letter

But how are we to develop that friendship with the Lord? After all, we can't see Him. How *can* you develop a friendship with Someone you can't see?

There are basically two ways. People who love each other can keep in touch, when separated, by writing letters and by using the telephone. You should see the students making a beeline for the letter rack in the morning or lining up outside the phone booth in the evening. If I were insensitive enough to ask them why they should think it worthwhile being late for their breakfast because they were eagerly fingering through the pile of letters in the hope that she might have written, or if I were tactless enough to inquire whether the nightly phone call to some faraway woman was worth the price of the call, the answer would be short and utterly sufficient: "Of course it's worth it. I love her."

It's like that with Christ. Before we came to know Him, we had no particular desire to get in touch, even if we believed in His existence. But now that we know Him and love Him, it's different. We shall want to use the letter and the phone. It won't be a dreary rule that we have to keep in order to develop a friendship. It will be the most natural thing in the world, for we love Him.

The Open Letter

Our Lord has in fact written an open letter to all members of His family. In it He tells them about Himself, about His plans for their good, about successes and failures of past members of the family, about love and self-discipline, about the family characteristics and the resources available to all the members. There are promises to claim, commands to obey, advice to note, prayers to echo, as well as examples to follow and warnings to heed. Best of all, this time of reading the Bible will warm your heart with love for your beloved Friend and strengthen your determination to please Him in the affairs of that day. It will become an important part of your life, this reading of His letter.

You will find, I think, that the Scriptures do not exaggerate when they describe their own function as food, without which we shall starve; as a sword, without which we shall be defeated; as a mirror, for lack of which we shall fail to see what we really look like; as a lamp, to shed light on our path; as a fire, to warm our cold hearts when they lose their glow; and as a hammer, to break the rock in pieces when we are being willfully disobedient (1 Pet. 2:2–3; Heb. 4:12; 2 Cor. 3:18; Ps. 119:105; Jer. 23:29). This book contains God's message for men and women, brought to us by the human writers, who themselves lived close enough to God to hear, assimilate, and interpret His will (2 Pet. 1:21). If you want to grow in your friendship with your Lord, you simply cannot afford to neglect it.

Does it look as if I am legislating? As if being a Christian involves a series of rules, of which one of the most important is "read your Bible daily"? No, that is not the case. There is no rule about it. But it stands to reason that if you love people, you will want to explore them fully, and if you can't see them and can communicate with them only by letter, you don't find it any hardship to study the letters! Sometimes Christians have become fixated on Bible reading. They have implied that unless you read it daily, and preferably before breakfast, you are going to make a mess of the day. Indeed, they have implied you are on the road to spoiling your friendship with Jesus.

There is a general reaction in Christian circles these days against such legalism, and rightly so. Jesus is not so mean as to withdraw His friendship if we skip reading the Bible for a day or two or three. But if it is true that the Bible is one of the main sources of nourishment for the Christian (and it is), ask yourself how well you would grow physically if you ate your meals at rare and irregular intervals. And if you react against the morning hour of traditional Christian devotion, ask yourself if it is because you are really at your best for your Friend later in the day, say in the evening—in which case, fine. Have it in the evening. Or is it because you are too idle to get up in the morning?

It may be a curious coincidence, but most great men and women of God in the past have found that if they didn't make time for Bible reading at the beginning of the day (for however short a time), they didn't make time at all. The rest of the day somehow seems to slip away. But you may be different. You may be iron-willed. You may be a busy homemaker who can get alone for half an hour after your spouse and the kids have gone off in the post-breakfast exodus. You may be the type who wakes up at night and is able to guard the last half hour of the day for being alone with your Friend. Get a time that suits you, and keep that special for Him. The important thing is that you should really meet with your Lord, not where or when you do it, or how long you spend at it.

How to Begin

Do you wonder, "How am I to go about it?" Perhaps the best advice would be to seek out Christian friends and ask for help in learning how to read a passage devotionally. It would be a good idea to meet them once a week for, say, a couple of months so that together you can study some chapters of the Bible that bear on the major aspects of Christian living. For instance, Luke 11:1–13 is a splendid passage on prayer, Ephesians 4:17—5:1 on Christian living, Romans 12 on Christian service. In such a regular, relaxed weekly meeting you can share with your friends the many teething troubles that come up in the early days of every Christian's experience. They have almost certainly had similar problems to face and are sure to be delighted to give you a hand. I personally found this weekly session with a more experienced Christian friend more help than anything else in developing my friendship with Christ.

But if no such friend is available, don't be discouraged. You have at your side One who will "never fail you nor forsake you" (Heb. 13:5). "You need no other teacher," wrote John, "for he teaches you all things, and he is the truth" (1 John 2:27). I would advise you to get a good modern translation of the Bible. There are lots of them. You would also be wise to get a regular system of reading it, or you may otherwise start at the beginning and get bogged down in the book of Numbers, or do a circular tour of your favorite passages!

But don't be afraid to change it later on if you feel in need of some variety. Perhaps branch out on your own. Sometimes you might read a whole book at a sitting: the book of Jonah, maybe, if you are feeling rebellious; or 1 Peter if you are going through tough times at work. Sometimes you might study a single verse intensively. For instance John 3:16, perhaps the most famous verse in the Bible, tells us of our great need: we are perishing, like someone drowning in a river. It speaks of God's great love: He gave Jesus to meet that need of people. And it speaks of a step of faith whereby all who believe may have God's new life. And by the time you have dug into a verse like that, you will find you have learned it by heart, and that may well prove very useful to you later on when you are trying to help other people.

More Ways than One

There are lots of other ways of Bible study. You can make a character study and trace the references in the New Testament to a man like Andrew who is mentioned only three times in the gospel of John, but on each occasion he is introducing someone else to Jesus. Or take one of the great heroes of faith in the Old Testament such as Abraham and see how he faced the temptation to take the easy course for fear of looking odd, the temptations to selfishness, to self-pity, and to water down God's promises. That man faced the same difficulties that come our way and more. The way he trusted God long ago can inspire and teach us today.

Alternatively, you may study a theme: what the Bible has to say about money, work, marriage, or faith, or perhaps what was the message and what were the qualities of the early Christians who had such striking success in the ancient world. As a change, you could take a single chapter and see what its main teaching is. Romans 8 is a great chapter, with its assurance about a Christian's past, the present, and the future with Christ; so is 2 Timothy 2 with its seven distinctive pen pictures of a Christian worker. Or you can trace a single significant word such as *inheritance, faithful,* or *able.* I have discovered a great deal by investigating the Christian inheritance that God has provided, by considering areas where He is calling me to be faithful, and by reflecting on what He has pledged Himself able to do in and through me.

These are some of the different ways in which you can study that inexhaustible book, the Bible. But whether you are doing some exploration on your own, or following a system like that of the Scripture

Union, remember that you are coming to read the Bible for a quite specific purpose. For you it is not "The Bible as Literature" or "The Bible as History" or "Biblical Criticism." It is the Bible as God's love letter to you. So come to Him in prayer before you begin. Ask Him to bring it alive for you as you read and to speak to you through it. And then read it through and through again, looking for a promise you can claim, a warning you can heed, an example you can follow, a prayer you can use, or something you had never spotted before about your Lord and Friend.

Two-Way Traffic

This Bible reading is not one-way traffic. You will want to pause to thank God for some new truth that has struck you; to adore Him for some fresh insight into what He has done for you; to search your conscience over some requirement of His; to think out the implications of some promise you have read. Bible reading, in fact, leads naturally into prayer. The reading of His letter drives you to pick up the phone of prayer. I once asked a student who had come to the Christian life only a month earlier, "What is the greatest difference you have noticed?" Her reply was interesting: "I have begun to love praying. I sometimes go on for ages because I am really in touch." That girl had learned the meaning of prayer; it is talking with God. Talking with Him about anything and everything of concern to us:

friends, the job, time off, home relationships, future career, disappointments, joys, everything, including the day's timetable.

Prayer is assuredly not a matter of set words (though there is a real place for formal prayers in a church service so that all present can join in them) or of fixed times (though without fixed times our praying will become spasmodic and probably chaotic). It is the sharing of our lives with our Friend. Why do you think Christ died for us? To show us His love? Yes. To take responsibility for our sins? Yes. But supremely to share our lives with us. "He died for us in order that we might *live with him*" (1 Thess. 5:10), with all the barriers formed by unforgiven sin knocked away and with nothing between us to spoil the friendship.

The Phone of Prayer

The following letter came to me from a young woman who had been a dancer, a model, and a nanny. She has subsequently married a clergyman! When she wrote it she had been a Christian only a few months, and this is what prayer was beginning to mean to her:

When I pray, it is to get close to God, to thank him for all he has given me and done for me, and to praise him in his glory. To ask for strength to do his will, so that through my actions people will see him in me. To get so close in the quietness of the mind that God can tell me what he wants me to do for him. To ask for help for myself and all my friends and family and for this world and its sin. To ask for forgiveness and strength not to sin again. To talk quietly with my Friend and my God and tell him all my inner feelings that I could never share with anyone else.

That is the essence of prayer: talking with God. But it involves listening to Him, too. We aren't very good at this—at least I'm not. I tend to talk too much, and it is hard for Him to make His will known to me. You may be the same: so busy talking you don't realize that He may well be calling on you to visit that lonely person down the road, to take some fresh fruit to that person in the hospital, or not to be impatient with your children. It may be that there is a gift of money He wants you to part with or a word that would help the person you work with. So long as you will give Him the chance by listening to Him, it is up to Him to get through to you, is it not? I find that comforting. It is His responsibility to show me His will. It is mine to do it.

Finding a Structure

If you want a structure to build your prayers around, how about using the Lord's Prayer as a pattern? After all, that's what it's meant for (Matt. 6:9; "Pray *like this* . . .").

"Our Father"—come to Him with the confidence

of children in the family and thank Him for accepting you and making you welcome.

"Who art in heaven"—that keeps the perspective straight and stops us from getting overfamiliar with God. He is great, glorious, heavenly, and I am puny and should approach Him not only with intimacy but also with awe and reverence.

"Thy kingdom come"—pray for the extension of God's kingly rule in the lives of those in your circle (and wider) who do not give Him their allegiance.

"Thy will be done"—pray for God's will to be done in the lives of those who do know Him on earth, just as it is done in heaven. Here is the place to pray over the details of your day's schedule, to recall your special weaknesses, and to pray for your church and your Christian friends, as well as those who are serving the Lord overseas or seeking to extend His kingly rule in industry or in government.

"Give us today our daily bread"—here you can include prayer for all your physical needs. God is concerned about them and invites you to make them known to Him. The "daily bread" in the original Aramaic seems to have meant "the bread of tomorrow." Give us today a foretaste of the wedding feast in heaven! That takes up our physical needs but transcends them. It asks for all we need to spend our day as citizens of the kingdom.

"Forgive us"—we never get past the need to ask for forgiveness from the daily sins and failures that all of us fall prey to. Call them to mind. Confess them. And receive His pardon. And remember, as Jesus told His followers, that you must be willing to forgive those who wrong you if you are going to be able to enjoy God's pardon.

"Lead us"—how we need His guidance each day. Commit to Him any special problem concerning you at present, particularly anything that is going to put you to the test.

"Deliver us"—from the unwelcome attacks of the evil one today: temper, greed, lack of self-control, or whatever your particular weak points may be.

For I am handing over to You the kingly rule in my life today, Lord. I am looking to You for the power to live as a Christian in today's world. And I promise that I will hand back the credit to You directly and not take it for myself. "Thine is the kingdom, and the power, and the glory, forever. Amen!"

Keeping It Natural

This structure may well be a help in the special time you set aside for prayer. But friends do not talk only on fixed occasions! Christ is a friend, so turn to Him at odd moments in the day. Is there some specially nice meal you have enjoyed? "Thank You, Lord," you say, and there's no need to shut your eyes or to kneel down to say it. Or is it some pressing temptation that attacks you? "Lord, please give me Your strength." Or have you failed Him? Don't wait until the evening to get it put right. Tell Him at once. "Lord, I've let You down. I am so sorry. Please forgive me, and help me to learn from my mistake and to ask You for Your help when I am tempted to repeat it."

One final thing. Friendship is all the more delightful when shared. If you are out for the evening with some other Christians, why not spend a few minutes in prayer to the Lord before you break up? You are sure to feel shy to begin with because it will seem strange to talk to God out loud in your own words in the company of others. But why not? Break the sound barrier. Launch out, however haltingly, and you will not regret it. I think I get to a deeper level of fellowship with other Christians when praying with them in this way than at any other time.

There it is then. Christ is your friend. And friendships need to be cultivated. Make sure yours doesn't fall into disrepair through neglect. The letter and the phone are indispensable for absent friends if they are to keep in touch. And though the analogy is not exact (for Christ is not absent; He is wonderfully present with you always), the point holds good. You *must* keep in touch with Him and He with you, and the Bible and prayer are prime ways to do this.

5

A NEW ATTITUDE

1. THE PRINCIPLE—
PLEASING CHRIST

On Human Bondage

In this age when we are more sensitive about freedom than almost any subject, there are unmistakable signs that people remain in bondage. I received a letter from a man who was a habitual gambler. Even though it was wrecking his family life, even though it was driving him to bankruptcy, he could not stop it. He was enslaved. With you it may be something much less obvious than gambling. Swearing? Smoking? Alcohol? Drugs? Bad temper? Ambition? These things may begin with the thinnest of threads; but progressively they grip us; they inhibit our freedom and mold us into becoming the sort of people we don't want to be. We can't help ourselves. "The man who does wrong," said Jesus, "becomes a slave to wrong" (John 8:34).

Human nature hasn't changed since His day: we

still please ourselves. However subtly it is dressed up, however various the guises it takes, self-centeredness is the motivating factor in human life. "Thank you very much," we say, "but I'll please myself."

The Bible writers were well aware of this universal tendency and very honest about it: "Once we, too, were foolish and disobedient; we were misled by others and became slaves to many evil pleasures and wicked desires. Our lives were full of resentment and envy. We hated others and they hated us" (Titus 3:3 TLB). That is Paul's summary of the governing factor in human attitudes before Christ comes on the scene. Hear Peter; he is writing about the paradoxical situation whereby the advocates of the permissive society in his day found their freedom shackled by the very things they allowed themselves: "The very teachers who offer this freedom from restraint are themselves enmeshed by evil habit. For a man is slave to whatever controls him" (2 Pet. 2:19). Or notice the way James pitches into the rich and selfish monied classes of his day: "Listen! Hear the cries of the workers in your fields whom you have cheated of their pay. Their cries have reached the ears of the Lord of hosts. You have spent your life here on earth having fun, satisfying your every whim, and now your fat hearts are ready for the slaughter" (James 5:4–5).

Yes, men and women remain now what they were then, "lovers of pleasure, not lovers of God"

(2 Tim. 3:4). You, too, used to be like that, did you not?

But now you're a Christian. What is to be your governing attitude? Is it to be determined by endless rules? Ought you to go out and buy a textbook on Christian ethics? Should you be bound by the taboos of the Christian group you have gotten attached to? What is the right attitude for a Christian facing the practical and perplexing decisions of daily behavior?

A Christ-Centered Ethic

Mercifully, the basic attitude is very simple indeed. Simple, but difficult. As ever, you find your example in Jesus. The supreme ambition of His life was to please His heavenly Father. Was it a question of the timing of His plan? He waited till He was sure when the Father's "hour" had come. Was it the ultimate question of the manner of His death? "Not my will, but thine be done" (John 13:1; Luke 22:42).

"Christ didn't please himself," said Paul, with masterly understatement (Rom. 15:3). The implication for Christians is so obvious that it scarcely needs drawing. Our aim should be to please not ourselves but Him. He is like the general who has recruited us to His forces. "As Christ's soldier do not let yourself become distracted by worldly affairs, for then you cannot please the one who has enlisted you," said Paul (2 Tim. 2:4). When in doubt about the rightness of some course of action, "we cannot just go ahead and please ourselves. Let's please the other fellow, not ourselves, and do what is for his good and thus build him up in the Lord" (Rom. 15:2). The subject specifically under discussion by Paul in that chapter is whether Christians should be vegetarians or not. His principle, however, is a fundamental one: we should please Christ and act as His responsible agents in society.

And that is really all we need to know about Christian ethics! For we are not shackled to a code of conduct but are responsible to a person, Jesus Christ Himself. Our motivation is not the stiff upper lip of duty but the gratitude of those who have been set free. How does Paul pray for Christians at Colossae, whom he has never seen? I guess he would pray for us in precisely the same terms, and it couldn't be bettered:

> Ever since we first heard about you we have kept on praying and asking God to help you understand what he wants you to do; asking that the way you live will always please the Lord and honor him, so that you will both be doing good, kind things for other people and at the same time getting to know God better and better (Col. 1:9–10).

There in a nutshell you have the revolution that underlies all truly Christian behavior. My main ambition is no longer to please myself but to please Him. Once pleasure was king. Now Jesus is King. Just think for a moment what that involves.

The Freedom It Brings

It gives full play to our freedom. The church, alas, has not always been noted for its advocacy of freedom. It has been unduly conservative about its traditions, timid in allowing Christian people their heads, and not infrequently committed to policies of reaction rather than reform. But when it has acted in this way, it has done so in straight contradiction to the New Testament. There we read such sentiments as these: "So Christ has made us free! Now make sure you stay free and don't get tied up again in the chains of slavery to laws and ceremonies" (Gal. 5:1). In this age, which is dedicated to the pursuit of freedom, Jesus offers us the key to freedom we could never enjoy without Him. A liberty to do what we know we ought; a liberty that is rooted deep within us as "the Spirit who brings new life in Christ sets us free from the downward pull of sin" (Rom. 8:2).

The Flexibility It Gives

There's another advantage in this Christ-centered ethic. It gives great flexibility. It means we are governed not by a set of unfeeling, unbreakable rules that we must keep but by a living, loving Person whom we aim to please. The focus of behavior is not external to us, a code of conduct we are expected to live up to: it is internal, as the Holy Spirit first helps us to *want* to go Christ's way, and then enables us to work out that allegiance in the complexities of modern life (Phil. 2:13).

The Reflection It Demands

That leads to another important point. It means that you and I have to apply our minds to the question of behavior. There is no slick answer to what Christian action may be in any given circumstance. We can't even simply look at the New Testament and read the solution off the page. We need to see how the early Christians tried to please Christ in their day and situation, and then translate that attitude into today's terms.

This is even true of the Sermon on the Mount, where, if anywhere, Jesus seems to be laying down a new code of behavior for the members of the kingdom of God. Is He not legislating? Not really. To be sure, He tells us that if a man hits us on one side of the face, we should turn the other cheek. But are we to carry that out literally, without thinking about the principle behind it? If we actually do get clobbered by a man in a fit of temper, the fastest way to drive him really wild is to do a smart about-face and offer him the other cheek. Literal obedience to the command could completely destroy the principle behind the command. The principle in this case is one of nonretaliation. Right. We must work out how best to show nonretaliation when we are provoked. But the ways of doing so will be legion and may not include literally turning the other cheek. Thank God, we are called not to obey a code of rules but to please a Person. Fulfilling that aim will amply engage our minds, our wills, and our attitudes to Christ.

The Variety It Allows

It also means that there will be a number of variations in the way Christians work out their faith in life. Let nobody persuade you that there is only one Christian attitude to disputed issues. There may well be several. Thank goodness, God is not interested in dull uniformity. Return for a moment to the New Testament church and see how Paul handled diversity in Christian practice. Some of the Christians at Rome and Corinth would not eat meat that had been offered to idols for fear they should tacitly seem to condone idolatry. Others said, "It can't do any harm. These idols don't exist. We have one Lord and Master, and He has given us food for our good. I shall eat it and be grateful." Diversity in Christian practice, then, from people who interpret the will of the Lord differently on this matter. But notice how wisely Paul handles it:

Don't criticize a brother Christian for having different ideas from yours about what is right and wrong. For instance, don't argue with him about whether or not to eat meat that has been offered to idols. . . . Those who think it is all right to eat such meat must not look down on those who won't. And if you are one of those who won't, don't find fault with those who do. For God has accepted them to be his children. They are God's servants, not yours. They are responsible to him, not to you (Rom. 14:1–4).

In point of fact, he goes on, God is pleased with both attitudes, conscientiously held as they are: "The man who eats meat eats it as a gift from the Lord, and he thanks God for it. The man who refrains from eating does so out of anxiety to please the Lord, and he too is thankful" (Rom. 14:6).

What a splendid, liberal, and responsible approach to ethics! Splendid because it is so humane. Liberal because it takes full account of the priceless gift of Christian freedom. Responsible because it anchors Christian behavior in all its variety to pleasing Jesus, the supreme pattern for human beings.

The Joy It Brings

Mention of Jesus reminds us that there is nothing cramping or burdensome about Christian morality. God does not want to make life dull and dreary for us; He wants to make it full to the brim and overflowing to those who do not know Him. To please Him is not restrictive; on the contrary, it is to take our proper place in creation whose very existence is to fulfill His will and do His pleasure. The will of God is not arbitrary; it is "good and acceptable and perfect" (Rom. 12:2 NRSV). Just because it is perfect, it is acceptable; we need not feel there is anything limiting in seeking to follow that will. It is nothing less than the very best purpose of God for us, the children He has brought into new life.

Such, then, is the revolutionary attitude brought about by Jesus. Freedom from evil habit through the indwelling of the Liberator. Freedom from rules and regulations through loyalty to Jesus. Freedom from smugness about our achievements, both because no one can be smug about responding to love and because there is still so much more to be attempted for Him. Freedom from a critical attitude toward the way other Christians work out their obedience, remembering that they may discern the will of the Lord more clearly than ourselves, and that variety can be honoring to God providing it stems from a genuine desire to please Christ. Yes, the Christian ethic is certainly liberating.

That, then, is the proper attitude: to ask, "What would please Christ? What would He do in my situation? What action on my part is likely to bring credit to Him?" Now let's be very practical and apply this principle to a single example, money. We'll look at a broader field in the next chapter.

2. THE APPLICATION— ONE EXAMPLE

The God of Wealth

Money is god for a great many people. It is taken for granted that we should get as rich as we can, and that the more we have, the happier we shall be. An improved standard of living is the goal of political parties of the Right and of the Left. What difference is being a Christian going to mean in this highly sensitive area of money?

The Jesus we follow was remarkably unconcerned about acquiring money. He appears to have been so poor that He had to borrow a coin when asked a question about tribute money. When required to pay it, He was glad to find a coin wedged in a fish's mouth. He was prepared to trust His heavenly Father for His needs. This did not mean that He was not equally prepared to work as a carpenter for His pay and, no doubt, to live off the proceeds of the catch when He went out with His fishermen friends. There was no doctrinaire opposition to money in Jesus of Nazareth; but no slavery to it, either. To be sure, He advised one rich young man to go and get rid of his cash, but He did not ask that of everybody. It is clear that money was standing between that man and discipleship. He was unwilling to let Jesus touch his pocket. And until He was allowed in there, Jesus could do nothing with that rich young ruler. "No man can serve two masters," as He said on another occasion. "You cannot serve God and money" (Matt. 6:24).

The Love of Money

No, there is nothing wrong with money, but there is a great deal wrong with the love of money (1 Tim. 6:10). Greed, oppression, avarice, dishonesty, fraud, robbery, and often murder as well, all spring from this love of money. And there's a curious, twofold irony about it. First, money does not satisfy. As the Romans recognized long ago, money is like seawater: the more you have of it, the thirstier you get. And second, money does not last. Jesus spoke of the moth and rust that spoil the possessions of those who go for money on earth. Today, income taxes, inflation, and the vagaries of the stock market replace moth and rust! But even if our fortune survives those hazards, it won't survive death. It is very short-lived. I remember talking to a woman who had nursed a man so rich that the ordinary cups in his house were made of silver. She discovered that it did not make him any the less miserable as he lay dying. The one certainty about our wealth is that we shall leave it all behind.

Don't be a fool, will you? It is not crucial that you make that extra pile of cash or get that overseas holiday. It doesn't matter that the Joneses have a swimming pool and you haven't. And don't envy your friend's sports car: it is only a status symbol. Surely you aren't in need of any such boost to your ego?

You may be poor all your days, but you are *rich:* you're heir to a kingdom.

Money—Our Security?

First, we shall not trust in our money. This is one of the most insidious dangers in wealth: it tends to make people arrogant, independent, and unwilling to rely on God for their needs; they have such a big bank balance, they don't feel they need to trust anyone. And you don't have to be rich to trust in money. It's just as big a danger to poor people. They are tempted to feel that if only they had money, all would be well, and they would have the security they have always lacked. Poor and rich people alike need to remember that the Christian has one security only, God. In poverty or wealth I am His and He is mine, and that is enough.

"Don't always be wishing you had more money," writes the unknown author of the letter to Hebrew Christians. "Be satisfied with what you have. For God has said, 'I will never, never fail you nor forsake you'" (Heb. 13:5). One Christian friend of mine, himself very poor, had his few choice possessions stolen from a friend's locked car. "No matter," he wrote. "They are welcome to my stuff. But praise God, they cannot take Jesus from me." And he meant it! I believe that if Christians were less attached to their possessions and more ready to trust God over their finances, the effect on society would be tremendous. It would stand out in striking contrast to the prevailing attitudes on both sides of industry, and also to those of the man or woman in the street.

Money—to Get or to Give?

Second, we shall want to give. This is all part of the inner revolution begun when the Spirit enters our lives. When Jesus was asked into the home of Zacchaeus, the notorious tax gatherer, the effect was electric. Zacchaeus was so magnetized by Christ's generosity that he said, "Sir, from now on I will give half my wealth to the poor, and if I find I have over-charged anyone on his taxes, I will penalize myself by giving him back four times as much." Jesus' comment is instructive: "This shows that salvation has come to this home today" (Luke 19:1–9). One of the yardsticks of a person's conversion is the change in the attitude to possessions.

Some years ago I was speaking at a conference in Jerusalem. One of the members had lost her luggage en route. In it she had packed a good deal of Christian literature written in both Hebrew and Arabic for free distribution in Jerusalem. Efforts to trace it failed until the last day, when it turned up damaged but with its contents intact. Indeed, there was one addition—a note from the thief who had stolen it. It read as follows:

I stole this from you because I was a thief, but after reading your cards I decided that your way, the way of the Lord, was the only way. So I am returning this to you and returning to the ways of

the Lord. You have saved my soul, and I am now
high on his way. Bless you.

I don't know whether that man had a sense of
humor, but he added this slight misquotation from
the Gospels to his letter of restitution:

> Seek and ye shall find.
> Take and ye shall receive.

Well, he had taken unlawfully and had received far
more than he ever imagined. So immediately it
affected his attitude to money. No longer was "finders
keepers" his rule. Greed had been deposed by God in
his life. The mark of a saved soul was a theft restored.
It spoke volumes about the inner change in the man.

That, I suppose, is what Paul had in mind in these
very illuminating words of advice to recent converts
at Ephesus: "If any of you have been stealing he
must stop it and begin using those hands of his for
honest work, so that he can give to others in need"
(Eph. 4:28). The one whose philosophy had been all
"get" now begins to give. The man who stole from
others because he had been too idle to work now
works to be able to give to others. How about that
for a new attitude?

Money—Our Right?

Third, we shall see ourselves as accountable to
God for our use of money. Hear Paul on the subject.

He must have been rich at one stage, or he could not have been a Roman citizen. He wrote,

> Tell those who are rich not to be proud and not to trust in their money, which will soon be gone, but their pride and trust should be in the living God who always richly gives us all we need for our enjoyment. Tell them to use their money to do good. They should be rich in good works and should give happily to those in need, always being ready to share with others whatever God has given them. By doing this they will be storing up real treasure for themselves in heaven—it is the only safe investment for eternity! And they will be living a fruitful Christian life down here as well (1 Tim. 6:17–19 TLB).

Whether I have a lot of money or a little is immaterial. As a Christian, I ought to give a proportion of my income to God. The Jews used to give 10 percent, and I do not see how a Christian can give less (even if a pensioner or a student on a grant!). But characteristically, the New Testament does not lay down any amount or even any proportion. For giving is not so much a duty as a highly personal demonstration of our love to the Lord.

Paul could write of the Christians in Macedonia,

> Though they have been going through much trouble and hard times, they have mixed their wonderful joy with their deep poverty, and the result has been an overflow of giving to others. They

gave not only what they could afford, but far more; and I can testify that they did it because they wanted to, and not because of nagging on my part (2 Cor. 8:2–3 TLB).

Naturally enough: "For you know the love and kindness of our Lord Jesus: though he was rich, yet to help you he became poor, so that you, through his poverty, might be rich" (2 Cor. 8:9).

That was Christ's attitude. Not surprising that it rubbed off on His followers. It still does. I think of a carpenter who had found Christ and pressed a sum of money into my hand at Christmastime shortly after his conversion. "Use it for the poor," he said. I think of an able young architectural student who celebrated his discovery of Christ by giving up his compulsive smoking and sending me a check to use in Christian work with the money thereby saved. Giving comes naturally to the heart that has responded to the giving of God. Too often church financial needs are tackled at the wrong level, it seems to me. "Give to save our old church" inspires nobody. But "Give because Christ gave Himself for you" is a very different matter.

Money for Sharing?

One of the strongest ways of demonstrating the supranational character of the Christian church is the loving contributions members make for fellow Christians in other parts of the world. Whenever there is a disaster, Christians are among the first to supply aid. Guatemala, Haiti, Bangladesh, Ethiopia, Poland, Uganda—in all these places Christians from other lands have put their money where their mouths are. It is impossible to neglect human need if you are a Christian. John said, "How does God's love abide in anyone who has the world's goods and sees a brother or sister in need and yet refuses help?" (1 John 3:17 NRSV).

Nor is it necessary to leave Christian relief work to the official agencies like Compassion International, TEAR Fund, and Christian Aid. The church I served in Oxford sent three of its members for preaching and teaching in Uganda, and they went with many hundreds of dollars' worth of provisions and other necessities provided by the members of the congregation. On another occasion a single woman on a fixed income was so overwhelmed by the needs in Poland that she mobilized help from all over the city of Oxford, stored the provisions in the church building, and then took a convoy to Poland herself. Money and possessions are for sharing.

Jesus had a special concern for poor and needy people. He told His followers that when they were meeting the needs of sick and poor people, the outcasts and the prisoners, they were in a very profound sense ministering to Him (Matt. 25:34–40). The disciples took this to heart. The first Jewish Christians in Jerusalem were not too busy preaching Jesus as the Messiah to organize relief for widows and orphans. The first gentile Christians in Antioch were not too preoccupied with their extensive missionary work to mount a famine relief fund for their stricken brothers and sisters hundreds of miles away in Jerusalem.

It is an interesting and significant fact that the New Testament writers use the same word, *koinōnia*, for "fellowship" and for "financial contribution." The two are not unconnected! One of the most moving examples I have known of Christians giving in order to express fellowship was in western Africa. There was civil war in Nigeria, and the Christians on both sides showed a love that transcended tribal loyalties and the peculiarly bitter feelings generated by civil strife. The moment the war ended, Christians led the way in the generous giving and receiving of financial aid. Their nationalism said, "Hate the other side and show that hate by fighting." Their Christianity said, "Love the other side and show that love by giving." Their Christianity prevailed over their nationalism. Freely they had received from Christ. Freely they gave. That's what Jesus would do, isn't it?

And That's Just the Start

Let's leave the subject of money there, though the New Testament writers have a lot more to say about it—appropriately enough in view of its importance. They certainly do not share our coyness in talking about the proper use of money. They tell us, for instance, not to judge other people by their money and their clothes, and not to dress extravagantly or eat luxuriously when others are in need. They tell us that we have a responsibility to be scrupulously fair and generous toward any people we employ, remembering that we have an Employer in heaven. They tell us that we are duty bound to make provision for our family if humanly possible. Remember how Jesus provided for His mother even when He was dying on the cross? Paul says bluntly, "The man who does not make provision for his own family is worse than an unbeliever" (1 Tim. 5:8). They tell us that we can invest our money in lives by contributing to the cause of the gospel throughout the world. They remind us that not only the proportion of our income that we give directly to God belongs to Him—so does the rest. How about your will, by the way? Are you planning to leave all your money to the family—or to leave some of it to Christian work? We are accountable to Him for the way we use our money. It is only lent to us. We act as administrators of Another's possessions.

You see how the Lord refuses to be boxed away in one little corner of our lives labeled "religious"? He wants to lay His honest, loving, unselfish hand on the whole thing. Work out the details for yourself— such is your Christian freedom. I have certainly found it a rewarding and somewhat shattering experience to study what guidelines the New Testament has to give on this question of pleasing Christ in our financial affairs. But it is tremendously liberating to realize that all we have and are is His, and to use our resources deliberately and joyfully for Him.

Of course there will be differences in the way Christians work out in practice that loyalty to Christ. There are no hard and fast rules. I think of one man who works in the stock exchange and yet is utterly surrendered to Christ in his use of money. I think of another who knows that for him financial obedience to Christ means having no assured income and working for a faith mission in the Philippines. In both men, despite the enormous differences, there is the same revolutionary principle at work: the principle of give, not get, of pleasing Christ, not self, in this matter of money. And that is what matters.

In this chapter I have taken money as just one example of the new attitude a Christian begins to adopt. But the principle of pleasing Christ applies equally to all the other areas of life. We shall be looking at three of them in the next chapter.

6

SILENT REVOLUTION

Some years ago I remember being struck by a remarkable film title. It was this: *Start the Revolution Without Me!* It seemed to me that the Christian life is the very opposite of this and consists of the new believer saying to Christ, "Start the revolution within me!" That is certainly what He does. It is a gradual revolution in most cases—no overnight coup. But over the course of a few years there is no doubt about it. We find we have been revolutionized inside.

We examined in the last chapter the basic Christian attitude of pleasing Christ. And we saw an example of the way this works out in our finances. In this chapter we shall select three other important areas of life to illustrate something more of the change Christ makes.

1. SEX

How Free Is Free Sex?

Let's begin with possibly the biggest area where Christian behavior will run counter to the current of today's society. It is taken for granted by many people these days that sexual love is the most important thing in life—perhaps the only thing that gives life meaning—and that we are entitled to pursue it as and where we can.

However, even the advocates of free sex are finding that everything in the garden is not so lovely. For one thing, the pleasure doesn't last. The trouble is that the act of sex can become separated from a lasting relationship between the people involved. And that dehumanizes sex and demoralizes those who do it. Roger McGough has caught this spirit of bitter disillusionment on the morning after in his poem "The Act of Love":

> The Act of Love lies somewhere
> Between the belly and the mind
> I lost the love some time ago
> Now I've only the act to grind
>
> Brought her back from a party
> Don't bother swapping names
> Identity's not needed
> When you're only playing games
>
> High on bedroom darkness
> We endure the pantomime
> Ships that go bang in the night
> Run aground on the sands of time
>
> Saved in the nick of dawn
> It's cornflakes and then good-bye

Another notch on the headboard
Another day wondering why

The Act of Love lies somewhere
Between the belly and the mind
I lost the love some time ago
Now I've only the act to grind

Of course, the unsatisfactory nature of mere physical sex is widely admitted by advocates of permis-
siveness. Robert Chartham, in his sensational sex
book *The Sensuous Couple*, begins by maintaining
that "physical sex should be a visible, tangible
expression of the emotional love the partners have
for one another," and "If you make love only for the
physical experience you are downgrading both
yourself and your partner to the behaviour of the
barnyard." He protests that lovemaking should pre-
vent you from being selfish. But the rest of the book
goes on to talk blithely about the variety of partners
emancipated lovers will have! What has happened
to the unselfishness? The woman is jettisoned and
another takes her place. For all his talk of consideration for his partner, Chartham's sophisticated
eroticism is just as selfish, just as subpersonal as the
quick job in the back of a car that he despises.

Christ's Attitude

What would Christ say to all this? We are fortu-
nately left in no doubt. He quotes the Old Testament
on the whole purpose of marriage and sexuality: "It

is written that at the beginning God created man and woman, and that a man should leave his father and mother, and be forever united to his wife. The two shall become one—no longer two, but one!" (Matt. 19:4–6 TLB). In other words, marriage is for keeps, and God's intention is that the sexual relationship should be the uniting bond between two partners throughout their married life. Fornication is out. Adultery is out. That is what Jesus stood for. That is what the early church stood for. Christians are committed to it.

What's Wrong with Sex Outside Marriage?

Now why this very tough line? Because love, marriage, and sex are meant to go together by the One who invented all three. Sexual intercourse is the closest possible relationship you can have with any other person, and the Maker's intention is that you use it as an outer symbol of the inner love you have for that other person: a love that, like God's own love, is fully personal, does not act selfishly, and does not give up. What passes for love in these casual liaisons is often depersonalized, frequently selfish ("how much can I get out of it?"), and normally short-lived, leaving behind it disillusionment and loneliness as the erstwhile partner is discarded on the human scrap heap.

What happens when the Maker's instructions are neglected? We have seen plenty of the bitter fruits of free sex in the past decade. It is a plain flouting of the will of God. It carries with it a sense of guilt. It frequently has to be covered up by lies and hypocrisy. It dehumanizes sex and makes it into an act in itself, separable both from a relationship and from a person. It causes traumas to the personality of those jettisoned, and a hardening in the attitudes of the "notch on the headboard" man. It artificially separates sex from love, fidelity, companionship, and children. It takes something that can never be returned. It betrays an inability to control our instinctive drives. And it undermines trust. The man who cannot be trusted to master himself before marriage cannot be trusted to do so in marriage. Inevitably the woman he eventually marries (whom, hypocritically, he would like to be a virgin!) will have to live with the gnawing doubt, "Will he remain faithful when my back is turned?" And what sort of a foundation for marriage is that?

Indeed, there are few things so disruptive of personality, home life, and society as unrestrained sensuality.

Even Masters and Johnson, the celebrated American sexologists, have come to the conclusion, after endorsing the permissive lifestyle for decades, that the only lastingly satisfying sexual relationships are those between one man and one woman for keeps. And they are certainly guided by no Christian persuasion—merely by observing in detail what happens when the Maker's instructions for the use of sex are flouted.

It's not because Christians are against sex that they so strongly endorse chastity before marriage and fidelity in it; on the contrary, it is because they value it so highly. Sex is too good a gift of God to cheapen. It is no mere animal coupling, but the deepest way in which two people can express mutual self-giving. It serves not only to symbolize but to deepen and enrich the unity and love between the partners. It is fun. It is satisfying. It is exhilarating. But take it away from the context of marriage, and it becomes dishonest. For it isolates one type of unity, sexual unity, from the other areas of self-commitment that are meant to go with it. It is acting a lie. That is why the New Testament is so strongly against extramarital sex. It separates what God has joined together—sex on the one hand, and lasting companionship, love, and self-giving on the other.

Subsidiary Questions

Once you take your stand on this, many of the other sexual questions are not so very difficult to answer. Should any variety of sex play be enjoyed by Christian couples? Why not, within the marriage bond? How can any practice be wrong that deepens the delight of the couple in each other?

Should contraception be practiced? Why not, provided it is done within marriage and in order responsibly to space children, not selfishly to avoid having them? Indeed, the appalling overpopulation of the world makes contraception no longer a questionable matter but a plain duty. We can thank God that just at the very moment in history when it has become so necessary, technical advances have made it so simple.

How about homosexuality? This is a highly complicated question requiring expert advice, perhaps from an experienced Christian doctor. The Bible is very clear that the practice of homosexuality is wrong, just as the practice of fornication is wrong. You may have a physical and psychological makeup that attracts you to members of your own sex in the same way that most people are attracted to the opposite sex. This problem can often respond to treatment. But it is possible for people with homosexual inclinations to refrain, through the power of Christ, from homosexual intercourse, just as it is possible for unmarried heterosexuals to abstain from heterosexual intercourse. You can't stop birds from flying over your head, as the old Chinese proverb has it, but you can stop them from nesting in your beard!

How about sexy literature and films? If this stuff arouses you, you are making things difficult for yourself by indulging in it. Erotic literature may be a legitimate stimulus to lovemaking for the married couple, but it is a cancerous growth in the mind of the unmarried Christian. If you're one who suffers from vertigo, don't see how close you can get to the edge of the precipice. Steer well clear!

How about masturbation? This used to be the

unmentionable sin of Victorian literature, the thing that sent you mad, the thing that could be overcome only by much exercise and cold baths. Now it is commonplace. What is the Christian, with the new attitude of pleasing Christ, to make of this? Well, it is selfish and habit-forming, and it leaves you feeling rather dissatisfied and ashamed. Yet it is nowhere expressly forbidden in Scripture, it has no lasting ill effects, and it is a much less harmful way of dealing with the over-weening sexual urges of adolescence than sexual experimentation with others. Can you do it with an uncondemning conscience? That is the question: "Happy is the man who does not condemn himself for what he allows himself to do" (Rom. 14:22). If not, it must go. And Christ the Liberator can break its grip.

Pornography

There remains that controversial matter of pornography. Controversial because nobody has succeeded in giving a foolproof definition of porn. Controversial because nobody can prove whether people are depraved by pornography or go for it because they are depraved. Controversial because legislation against it would limit the liberty of the individual (though you have only to apply that argument to race relations to see the fallacy in it!). What is beyond controversy is that to separate sex-uality as a sort of cult object, in isolation from lasting relationships and as the supreme goal of human desire, is out for the Christian. Bishop Trevor Huddleston once put the Christian view very succinctly:

> The Christian religion takes its stand on the dignity of man, because it proclaims that man is made in the image and likeness of God. It goes even further than that. It proclaims that God himself has become man, and has, therefore, given a dignity to man which is infinite. Pornography is a symptom—it isn't a disease in itself. It is a symptom of a sick society. It's the consequence of society's thinking about the final end of man. It is the substitution of what, in truth, is the final end of man (namely the vision of God and the glory of God) by a limited and totally inadequate conception of what man is made for. Flowing from this real misunderstanding of what man is created to be in this world comes the idea that you can use the human body for a purpose which is wholly trivial. And this is what pornography does. Putting it crudely, you are substituting lust for love.

He continued the broadcast from which this quotation is taken by calling on Christians to be prepared to face the opposition this emphasis on chastity will bring. "Marvel not if the world hates you. It hated me before it hated you," was Jesus' comment on the inevitable difficulty of swimming against the current of society, which is at odds with

God (John 7:7). Huddleston concluded, "In fact purity of heart, chastity, lies at the very center of the gospel, and if we preach the whole gospel then we are bound to preach purity of heart."

2. SUFFERING AND DEATH

The Problem of Pain

If sex is the main preoccupation of our thoughts when we are younger, pain and death take over the top positions when we grow older. Just as sex is regarded by our society as the best thing in life, death is universally held to be the worst disaster that could overtake us, and suffering the next worst.

One thing we can be sure of. Pain and death will come our way. How does being Christian alter our attitude to them? You have only to visit in a hospital to hear questions like these: "Why should this happen to me? What have I done to deserve this? How could God allow it?" We shall be better able to face suffering when it comes if we have done a bit of thinking about it beforehand.

The problem of pain is an intractable one: nobody has gotten to the bottom of it, and nobody will. We need not, however, be embarrassed by this. The Christian faith enables us to see suffering in a more positive light than any other religion or philosophy in the world.

Why Does God Allow It?

Let's be clear about this to start with. The Bible makes it very plain that God wants the utmost good for His creatures. Suffering and pain are never the direct will of God for us. He may permit them, but He does not send them: "He does not willingly afflict the children of men" (Lam. 3:33). There are, however, four limitations on God's designs for our good.

First, there is the nature of our planet. It is consistent. It works to regular laws. And that is just as well, or we should never know where we were! But it means that if a knife will cut bread, it will also cut my finger. The useful force of gravity, which keeps me on this earth, is not suspended for my benefit when I fall out of the window. So at least the possibility of pain is built into the very structure of our world, where cause and effect prevail. This is inevitable; it is also invaluable. Pain can be nature's red light of warning. Were it not for the pain given by an inflamed appendix, it would burst inside you, and you would die.

Second, there is the existence of Satan. The Bible is quite clear about the reality of this anti-God force, the devil, and I would have thought that there was plenty of evidence the world over to show that he is still in business. But the Bible is equally clear that the devil is not an equal and opposite figure to God. There is no dualism here. The devil remains "God's devil," as Luther called him: he is on a chain, albeit a long one. His eventual destiny is destruction, but in the meantime he is out to spoil God's world in every way possible. He spoils personal life by sin, family life by discord, social life by greed, national life by war—and physical life by disease. Although making it clear that individual illness is not the result of individual sin, Jesus left us in no doubt that the devil has a hand in disease. When He healed one woman on the Sabbath day, He referred to "the bondage in which Satan had held her for eighteen years" (Luke 13:16). And in Acts we read of the way in which Jesus had healed "those who were oppressed by the devil" (Acts 10:38). This is one aspect of suffering we do well to take note of. There is a devil, and he is out to spoil.

Third, there is the fact of human free will. This is a major cause of pain in the world. God cannot take away freedom from people when they use it to reject His way for them. That would be to reduce them to robots—and He is love. Love can't be satisfied with robots. No, God will not intervene to stop train accidents, wars, thalidomide babies, and the other products of human misuse of freedom. Let's make sure we don't blame God for these things.

But that does not cover all pain: it does not explain hurricanes and earthquakes. There is, therefore, *a fourth factor* we must take into account. It is *the interdependence of a fallen world.* The world is not as God meant it to be. The Architect's plans have been scrapped by His clients. Chaos has resulted. And it affects every aspect of our rebel world. In the picturesque account of Genesis, the act of human disobedience results not only in shame, alienation from God, and banishment, but in the disruption of nature with thorns and thistles. We and our environment belong together, as we are all belatedly discovering. Human rebellion has affected our habitat. We are not just individuals: we are part of a common humanity, and it is tainted stock.

When you come to think of it, the sheer randomness with which suffering strikes is not so surprising after all. It is rather like smallpox. Once the virus has infected your bloodstream, the actual spots occur quite at random. There will be no rhyme or reason to their appearance. It is like that with suffering in the body of humanity. It does strike at random. It is no good asking, "Why should this happen to me?" any more than we ask with smallpox, "Why should this spot occur here?" In both instances the disease has to be met at its root. Suffering as a whole is linked with human sin as a whole: though individual suffering is not by any means necessarily related to individual sin.

What Has God Done About It?

Well, what has God done to meet the problem at its root? The Cross is the deep and mysterious but wonderful answer. And from the Cross these four beams of light shine out upon our problem.

First, the Cross shows that God is no stranger to pain. He does not allow us to go through what He

Himself avoids. He is the suffering God, the One whose royalty is displayed in suffering and in dying. "In all their distress he was distressed," the Old Testament says of God (Isa. 63:9 NRSV), just as a father agonizes over a sick child or a teenager's wild oats. But supremely He shared our agony on that cross. The Cross shows He knows all about suffering. The Cross shows He has been through it. And He still suffers in and with all the suffering of humanity. Ever since the Incarnation He has remained one of us. Isn't that just like God? He did not give us an answer to the problem of pain: He shared it. He did not explain it: He accepted it.

Second, the Cross shows that God loves on through pain. If you are ever tempted to feel that suffering is a sign God does not love you, remember that Jesus died on a cross, yet God still loved Him. It was into God's hand that Jesus committed His spirit. We can do the same, for we are not left desolate and unloved when we suffer. We may not understand the experience we are going through, but the cross of Jesus Christ assures us that God still loves us.

Third, the Cross shows how God uses pain. Evil though it is, God makes good come out of suffering in a variety of ways. He does it in nature. Think of the way an oyster uses the irritation of grit within the shell to turn it into a pearl. He does it in human character. Think of qualities like courage, self-sacrifice, and endurance that spring only from the soil of suffering. He does it in the spiritual life, too. Sometimes He uses pain to *reach* us. I have met several people who would never have stopped to listen to God and would never have come to know Him were it not for some tragedy that halted them in their tracks and made them think. Sometimes He uses pain to *teach* us:

> Let God train you, for he is doing what any loving father does for his children. Whoever heard of a son who was never corrected? If God doesn't discipline you when you need it, as other fathers do, it suggests you are not his true children at all, but illegitimate! (Heb. 12:6–8).

Sometimes He uses pain to *equip* us. Paul came to realize that a ghastly experience he had been through was intended by God to equip him to "comfort others with the comfort by which God had comforted him" (2 Cor. 1:4). So just think of the wonderful way in which God blessed and overruled for good the tragic agony of the Cross, and remember that He can and does use pain, though He does not will it.

Fourth, since the Cross can never be separated from the Resurrection, *it points to God's triumph over pain*. We have seen that pain as a whole is due to sin as a whole. On the cross Jesus dealt with sin at its root. He fought Satan and won. He bore sin and drew its fangs. He drained the cup of suffering and won through. Good Friday was followed by Easter Day. And we can look with sober confidence to a final triumph over pain because Christ has triumphed over sin, which caused it. Paul does so in a famous chapter of his letter to the Romans:

Since we are his children, we will share his treasures—for all God gives to his Son Jesus is now ours, too. But if we are to share his glory, we must also share his suffering. Yet what we suffer now is nothing compared to the glory he will give us later. For all creation is waiting patiently and hopefully for that future day when God will resurrect his children. For on that day thorns and thistles, sin, death and decay—the things that overcame the world against its will at God's command—will all disappear, and the world around us will share in the glorious freedom of the children of God.

For we know that even the things of nature, like animals and plants, suffer in sickness and death as they await this great event. And even we Christians, although we have the Holy Spirit within us as a foretaste of future glory, also groan to be released from pain and suffering. We, too, anxiously wait for that day when God will give us our full rights as his children, including the new bodies he has promised us—bodies that will never be sick again and never die (Rom. 8:17–23).

Such is the Christian hope. It is soundly based on the resurrection of Jesus Christ from the dead, the pledge of God's final triumph over sin and death.

A Note of Triumph

This means that we can face not only suffering but death in a new light. No longer will we see it as the worst thing that can befall us; no longer as the extinction of our lives. We shall see it rather as the door into a fuller life, a life that we shall continue to share with Christ as we share this life now. But a life that will not be marred by sorrow or suffering or decay. In his vision of heaven, John brings this point out with matchless poetry:

> I heard a loud shout from the throne saying, "Look, God shares his home with men. And he will live with them, and they will be his people and he will be their God. He will wipe away all tears from their eyes, and there shall be no more death, nor sorrow, nor crying, nor pain. All of that is gone forever" (Rev 21.3—4).

Away, then, with the gloom that so often accompanies even Christian funerals. The Christian dead go to "be with Christ, which is far better" (Phil. 1:23). Let us wear beautiful flowers in our buttonholes—not black ties—and rejoice—not go around with hushed voices. Let those who have no hope of heaven, no expectation of life after death, treat death as the last enemy if they must. But for us it is a defeated enemy, ever since the first Easter Day.

Of course there is shock. Of course there is loneliness for the one who is left. We must support bereaved people with great sensitivity. But for the departed Christian we can confidently rejoice. Let's have a bit more of this confidence and rejoicing as we grow older and face the somber realities of pain and death. We Christians are the only people in the world who have something to shout about at this point. Our Lord Jesus has been through it all; He has overcome. And when we go through the valley of the shadow, He will be with us; He will receive us. He has promised.

3. SELF-DISCIPLINE

If the youthful years of our Christian lives show a silent revolution in our attitude to sex, and the later years lead to a similar revolution in our attitude to suffering and death, Christians are called to face the current of popular attitudes in the matter of self-discipline throughout their lives.

It is an unwelcome subject. "Do your own thing" is the accepted norm. But if we love Him, we shall be prepared to do His thing. Self-control is really Christ-control because I certainly can't control myself. I need Him to do that. And in view of all He has done for me, I am prepared to let Him do so. Let's have a quick look at some of the areas it may involve.

Ambition

Some people aren't worried by this one at all, but others are eaten up by it. They must get to the top of their particular tree, whoever they have to step on in getting there. Well, this attitude will change once we're Christians. In some ways it is no bad thing to have a driving ambition—provided it is redirected. I shall no longer be out to show how wonderful I am, but I can channel all that drive into living my life to the fullest for Christ. I think of a general, of a financier, of an actor, all of whom belong to Christ, all of whom have laid their careers at His feet, all of whom want above all to please Him.

Paul was like that. Once he had been ambitious for himself; then he became ambitious for Christ. Listen to him:

> I was a real Jew if ever there was one! What's more I was a member of the Pharisees who demand the strictest obedience to every Jewish law and custom. And sincere? Yes, so much so that I greatly persecuted the church; and I tried to obey every Jewish rule and regulation right down to the very last point.

> But all these things that I once thought very worthwhile—now I've thrown them all away, so that I can put my trust in Christ alone. . . . I am bringing all my energies to bear on this one thing. Forgetting the past, and looking forward to what lies ahead, I strain to reach the end of the race and receive the prize for which God is calling us up to heaven because of what Christ did for us (Phil. 3:5–14).

Did you get that promotion? Then thank Him for the wider opportunities of service it offers. Did you get passed over? Don't take it to heart. It means the

Lord wants you where you are. You have only one life. You have given it over to Him for His safekeeping and His guidance. He knows what He is doing. He will give you the sphere of work in which the talents He has entrusted to you will be best deployed. So what are you worrying for? You don't have to prove anything by trying to show what a fine person you are. He has accepted you even though you are not nearly such a fine person as you thought.

The Lord has a place in His plan for you to work for Him. So pray about your work. Tell Him that you are willing to stay where you are or move on, just as He wishes. You'll find that you are delivered at a stroke from the burning ambition that eats up some of your fellow workers and gives them a chip on the shoulder if they are not successful or ulcers from overwork if they are. Make it your ambition to please Him. Never selfishly seek, or refuse, a position of greater responsibility. Your life is in better hands than yours. He knows what you were made for, and He will give you fulfillment in your work.

Time

This is an area where we are incredibly wasteful. How much time do you simply waste each day? It must be phenomenal, even for busy people. Of course, the Lord does not want us to be tense, overearnest killjoys, all work and no play. But He does want to guide us in the use of our time. After

all, we have only one life. Each day is an unrepeat-
able experience.

He lends us our time, just as He lends us our talents. And He wants to direct our use of it. Time for
Himself and deepening the friendship. Time for the
job. Time for the family. Time for Christian service.
Time for sleep is important: some of us have too
much, some too little. Find what you need, and try
to stick to it. There needs to be a balance, a whole-
ness about our use of time, so that we are not sloth-
ful on the one hand, or running around chasing the
clock on the other. "My times are in your hand"
wrote the psalmist (Ps. 31:15 NRSV). Let's ask His
guidance on this important side of our lives every
day, and His blessing on our use of it.

Leisure

This is worth a thought. The five-day week is
universal. The four-day week is on the way. The
amount of leisure will rocket. And masses of people
won't know what to do with it. Stupefying boredom
leaves millions gaping at the television set for hours
each evening. What will it be like in a few years?

But Christians won't be bored. We share our
leisure time, just as we share our work time, with
our Lord. And there is always something to be done
for others. I remember how, in the last year of his
long life, the saintly Bishop Houghton told me that
he walked down the road to the bus stop at eight
o'clock every morning with a schoolboy who lived

across the street—simply out of love for Jesus and the desire to share that love with the lad. That is the charm of the Christian life, or one of them. You never retire. You are never too old to be of use to your Friend: doing things for Him, introducing others to Him. The scope for Christian service in our leisure time is greater now than at any time in the history of the church.

Perhaps as a Christian you will want to review your vacation arrangements. More and more people spend an ever-increasing amount on overseas vacations when an equally restful time could be had nearer at hand at a quarter of the cost. At a time when world famine is greater than ever before, when missionary societies are more than ever pressed for funds, do we spend more on ourselves and our vacation arrangements than our Friend would wish? It may be worth talking over with Him.

Cigarettes, Alcohol, and Drugs

What is a Christian to do about these stimulants?

Nobody should rob us of our personal freedom in these matters. We have been called to liberty, and this is not the moment to reach for the rule book. Nevertheless, two limitations on our freedom are clearly given in the New Testament: "All things are lawful to me, but all things are not expedient. All things are lawful to me but I will not be brought under the power of any" (1 Cor. 6:12). That was one crucial question Paul asked himself: Are these perfectly legitimate things going to rob me of my freedom by bringing me into a new bondage, by gripping me in a habit I can't break?

The second question is this: What effect will the exercise of my liberty have on other people who may look to me for an example? "But why," you may ask, "must I be guided and limited by what someone else thinks? If I can thank God for the food [Paul's example is drawn from whether or not to eat food that had been offered to idols, but the principle behind it is widely applicable] and enjoy it, why let people spoil everything just because they think I am wrong?" "Well, I'll tell you why," says Paul.

> It is because you must do everything for the glory of God, even your eating and drinking. So don't be a stumbling block to anyone, whether they are Jews or Gentiles or Christians. That is the plan I follow, too. I try to please everyone in everything I do, not doing what I like or what is best for me, but what is best for them, so that they may be saved (1 Cor. 10:31–33 TLB).

Now apply these two principles to alcohol and cigarettes and drugs. Are you master of them, or are they master of you? Spurgeon reckoned he could smoke the occasional cigar to the glory of God, but many Christians who smoke are enslaved by it. I suppose the Christian attitude here is either moderation or none at all.

But then we have to take into account the second

question: What would others think? Would it or would it not commend our Master? One friend to whom I was speaking recently told me that as a chain-smoking, hard-drinking man he had cut it out completely when he became a Christian. On the building site where he worked they were amazed to find a real Christian. But having found him, they would have been even more amazed if he continued to drink and smoke. For him, therefore, it would have been wrong to continue. With you in your circumstances it may be different. It is something to put to Christ and let Him guide you.

It comes to this, really: Where do you intend to get your stimulus from? Christ—or drugs, alcohol, and cigarettes? If we are high on reality, the reality of Christ as our friend, we shall certainly not allow ourselves to be enslaved by any of these things. We may occasionally use them when the circumstances are right. But we will derive our main stimulus from elsewhere.

Listen to Paul again: "Don't drink too much wine, for many evils lie along that path; be filled instead with the Holy Spirit, and be controlled by him as you sing and make melody in your heart to the Lord" (Eph. 5:18–19).

Language

James wrote,

Men can train every kind of animal or bird that lives, but no human being can tame the tongue. It is always ready to pour out its deadly poison. Sometimes it praises our heavenly Father, and sometimes it breaks out into curses against men who are made in the likeness of God. And so blessing and cursing come pouring out of the same mouth. Dear brothers, surely this is not right (James 3:7–10).

No, of course it is not. The cruel words, the foul talk, the backbiting, the white lies, the half-truths, and all the rest of it. Jesus Christ wants our language to bring credit to Him. He is quite prepared to do the impossible and tame our tongues if we will make them over to Him. Paul expected to see the language of the converts at Ephesus change:

Don't use bad language. Say only what is good and helpful to those you are talking to, and what will give them a blessing. Don't grieve the Holy Spirit. Put all bitterness, anger and bad temper away. Quarreling, harsh words and malice should have no place in your lives. Instead, be kind to each other, tender-hearted, forgiving one another, just as God, for Christ's sake, has forgiven you. . . . Dirty stories, foul talk and coarse jokes—these are not for you. Instead, remind each other of God's goodness and be thankful (Eph. 4:29—5:4).

I like that last bit. Our minds are so constituted that we can't concentrate on two things at the same time. When the temptation to give way to foul talk hits you, try thanking God for His goodness, and you'll find the temptation withers away. Another thing I have found helpful is to pray the psalmist's prayer before each day begins—as I put on my clothes maybe: "Set a watch, O Lord, before my mouth. Keep the door of my lips" (Ps. 141:3). You'll find He can tame even that intractable member, the tongue.

In all these areas of life the silent revolution goes on, once Jesus is welcomed into our lives and made at home. So long as we make it our determination to please Him in all we do, we can safely leave the rest to Him. He has the power to transform us, and transform us He will, provided we are willing to be changed. But not otherwise. He declines to force His way upon us if we refuse Him entry to some area of our lives—if we say, in effect, "Start the revolution without me."

New Relationships

1. PERSONAL RELATIONSHIPS AT HOME

It was a dull afternoon, and I was watching him talk to the large number of older people who had gathered for their regular informal Thursday afternoon meeting. I was struck by the way he seemed to care. Then I met his wife, and I noticed their relaxed trust in each other and their obvious harmony. I remarked to my friend the vicar that he had a splendid new assistant, even if he was a bit older than most. Then he told me the story. Actually, I could not do better than give it to you in the assistant's own words:

> When I was in my early thirties, I became involved with another woman. I fell deep into sin—sin of the ugliest kind—which made me reject all thoughts of God and which very nearly broke up our family life. Five months in a neurosis [mental] hospital under the care of some of the finest psychiatrists made no difference to my attitude to life. I came out of hospital worse than

when I went in. I had developed a terrible stammer; I took drugs at night to try to help me sleep; I took pep pills during the day to try to keep me going; I went out of my way to avoid contact with anyone at all; I fainted in the streets and I jeered at anyone who tried to help me. I was determined to carry on with my selfish and sinful way of life, no matter what hurt it caused other people.

Then one Christmas, my son Alan (who was then just eight years old) gave me a picture of the Lord Jesus standing at the door, knocking. "Listen! I am standing at the door, knocking; if you hear my voice and open the door, I will come in to you and eat with you, and you with me" (Rev. 3:20 NRSV). For a long time I deliberately turned away from that picture. But the knocking became more and more insistent until finally, at 10:00 P.M. on the 26th June, 1961, in utter desperation and almost unbelief, I said, "Lord, you say you can change people's lives—come into my heart and change mine." At last I had taken that step of faith, and immediately my prayer was answered. There was a complete transformation in my life from that moment onwards.

Undoubtedly there was. It was perfectly obvious, even to the casual observer. Once devoted to self, he was now an ordained minister, giving himself for others. Once ruining his family life by a relationship with another woman, he was now happily reunited with his wife and at one with her in the work of the Lord. Once dependent on drugs for excitement, he was now alive with Christ's joy and love. Quite a change. And nowhere greater than in his relationships with others. It doesn't take much imagination to think what a different place his home is now.

And home is the place to begin. Jesus once healed a man who had serious psychological trouble. The man wanted to accompany Him as a disciple on a roving ministry. In a way that would have been much easier for him. But Jesus said, "No. Go back home to your folks, and let them know what wonderful things the Lord has done for you" (Mark 5:19). Christianity, like charity, begins at home.

It's the Life that Counts

I don't think it is wise to *talk* too much about Jesus at home to begin with. They know you too well! They will probably think you have a touch of religious mania, and that given time it will blow over. So softly, softly, as far as talking goes. Begin with living. Let your allegiance to Jesus show itself in a new cheerfulness around the house, particularly when others are in the dumps. A new helpfulness when the wife is obviously getting tired—how about *you* washing the dishes and doing the cleaning and putting the kids to bed? Or maybe you are one of the youngsters in the family. One of the best things you can do is to see that your room is not so knee-deep in mess that Mom can't get in to clean. "What, tidiness?" you say. "A boring virtue." Not when someone else has to come and clean up after you. It is a matter of Christian considerateness.

The scope for mutual considerateness in the home is enormous. We are called to "bear one another's burdens and so fulfill the law of Christ" (Gal. 6:2). Nowhere is burden bearing more sorely needed than in the home. Think of ways in which you can work out in family life the principle of pleasing Christ that lies at the heart of Christian living.

New Depth to Sharing

If both partners in the home have come to know Christ, this at once brings a new depth to their relationship. I vividly recall one evening when a couple, both of whom had given in, after a real struggle, to the claims of Jesus, said with tears of joy in their eyes: "This is more wonderful than our wedding day." At once they began to use their home for the Lord. They offered their place as a venue for one of the house meetings that was starting up in this parish, composed of some who had recently discovered the new life, and some who were still searching. It is a marvelous joy to use your home like that.

It is a wonderful thing for a Christian couple to go to sleep in each other's arms at night, having just shared the events of the past day, its joys and failings, with the Lord, and having committed to Him their lives and schedules for the next day. It is a wonderful thing to be able to pray with your children— and they so often have a shrewder insight and clearer perception of right and wrong than we do. God cares very much about the family: He invented it. Moreover, it is the fundamental unit in society. What we do as a Christian family, therefore, is more important than any other Christian work we attempt for God. If we fail here, we fail comprehensively. Many Christians make the mistake of neglecting their family responsibilities, either as children or as parents, in the interests of Christian service outside the family. It's a snare and delusion. Don't fall for it!

Open House

A Christian family will be a happy place: Jesus is welcomed in, and "in his presence is fullness of joy" (Ps. 16:11). It will be a hospitable place: "given to hospitality" was one of the characteristics of the early Christians, and it still marks out authentic Christianity. The home is not meant to be enjoyed in lonely isolation: it is there to be shared. This is hard work, but it is most rewarding, not only to the parents but also to the children. Once our daughter, age three, went to stay with her granny (who lives alone) and, when Sunday lunch arrived, said, "I need more people." She wanted to know where the students were. When Granny replied that no students were to be had, she piped up: "Then let's go out and buy some!" That child had some root of Christian hospitality planted firmly inside her!

I don't know what it is, but time and again people express their gratitude when they have been made to feel welcome in a Christian home. I would like to think it is something of the attractiveness of Jesus getting through. I remember an income-tax inspector's home I used to go to when I was in the army. It was years ago, but I have never forgotten it. This delightful Christian family used to open their home assiduously. If I ever wanted to help one of my army friends to find Christ, I used to take him for a meal and a chat there. They did not talk to him about Christ (unless he raised the subject), but their home radiated Christ's presence, softened him up, and generally led him to ask what it was those people had!

No Need to Pretend

Of course there will be arguments and failures in the Christian home. But they won't last long, because as members of the heavenly Father's family, they will quickly come to Him and apologize, and apologize to each other as well. "Do not let the sun go down on your anger" is sound biblical wisdom (Eph. 4:26 NRSV). It applies to husbands and wives (how can they pray together at night if they are holding something against the other?) and to parents and children. How important it is, by the way, that parents should not be too proud to apologize to their children. Yet too few do it. To Christians it will come naturally; we don't have to pretend we are better than anyone else. The fact that we have come to Christ for pardon means we are sinners, we know it, and we are not ashamed to admit it to even our nearest and dearest.

Halfway House

But how about the situation where the home cannot be called Christian—one partner is committed to Christ and the other is not? Tact, not talk, is the crucial thing. Don't be ashamed of your Friend, but don't embarrass others by constant reference to Him. There's a lovely piece of advice in 1 Peter for Christian wives married to unbelieving husbands: "Wives, fit in with your husbands' plans; for then if they refuse to listen when you talk to them about the Lord, they will be won by your respectful, pure behavior. Your godly lives will speak to them better than any words" (1 Pet. 3:1–2 TLB).

Above all, pray on for your loved ones. The fact that God has put you, a believer, in the same family as them is an indication that He wants to reach the whole family through you, His bridgehead. Your consistent life and your persistent prayer are likely in time to undermine the stoutest opposition.

I met in Canada recently the tough head of a building firm—now a radiant Christian. But it had taken six years of wise, loving, prayerful behavior on his wife's part before he gave in to Jesus. Or think of Saint Augustine—a licentious youth who traced his eventual conversion to the faithfulness of his mother's prayers.

Pray on for those in your family who are strangers to Christ as yet. Ask Him to shine through you as well as through your Christian friends who drop in. Expect things to happen. They will. I shall never forget meeting in Jerusalem an Arab girl who had been brought to Christ through the loving care of an Israeli Christian woman. The girl went back to her home and said very little about her faith in Christ, but she began to read the Bible and to pray. Her parents were curious to know what she was up to; they asked her, and before long they, too, had come to Christ.

Bleak House?

Some of you reading this may feel, "It's all very well talking about married people in their homes. I'm not married—and I haven't got a home." That may well be your position; but it needn't add up to a "Bleak House" situation. In the first place, remember that there are many things you can do and many places you can go for Christ as a single person that would be out of the question if you were married. That is why Paul wrote to the Corinthians in praise of the single state: "An unmarried man can spend his time doing the Lord's work and thinking how to please him. But a married man can't do that so well; he has to think about his earthly responsibilities and how to please his wife" (1 Cor. 7:32–33 TLB).

Second, it may well be God's purpose for you to be married and have a home later on, but not just now. Can't you trust Him to bring the right person across your path without fretting because friends of your own age have their partners lined up? God's plans are often for those who are prepared to wait.

But, third, it may be His will for you to be single.

Paul wrote about "some to whom God gives the gift of husband or wife, and others to whom he gives the gift of being able to stay happily unmarried" (1 Cor. 7:7). Both marriage and celibacy are *gifts* from the Lord. And though we may prefer the gift of marriage, that might not be God's perfect will for us.

Jesus commended those who "refuse to marry for the sake of the Kingdom of Heaven" (Matt. 19:12 TLB). That could be His calling for you. If it is, there is no need to lead an unfulfilled life. After all, Jesus remained a bachelor. Could anyone call Him odd, unbalanced, or unfulfilled? Several of my closest friends have remained unmarried for the Lord's sake, and their lives have been enriched by the sacrifice. Their hospitality to others and their talent for friendship have been enhanced by remaining single.

Others of my Christian friends have been bereaved at an early age and have suddenly found themselves single again. This is how one young mother is coping, whose husband died five years ago from cancer at the age of about thirty:

I'm getting used to having to make it on my own, and the Lord has been marvellously good to me. I have received so much in so many ways.

I think now I'm teaching, and I've joined the local choral society, I feel more of a complete person, if you see what I mean, though I still long for the day to day companionship of give and take. But even there I think I'm slowly learning to lean on God more.

Here is another letter, which shows the courage of a young clergyman whose wife died from an overdose of sleeping tablets, taken during a deep clinical depression to which she had been subject for some years. He has continued in his parish and writes,

> The Lord has been very real to me in the last few months, and the fellowship and hospitality of his people are absolutely wonderful. It is great to know it in experience as well as preach about it. This has been a year I will never forget, but one which I can look back on with thanksgiving as well as heartache. I'm indeed grateful for the advice to extract every positive aspect from the illness and passing of dear Jenny. With the Lord's help I am beginning to do just that. Life is very full, rich, and satisfying—as only the Christian ministry can be.

With Christ in the house it need not be bleak, even if, humanly speaking, you are on your own.

2. PERSONAL RELATIONSHIPS AT LARGE

At Work

It won't be long before the people at work realize that something has happened. They may wonder what makes you so happy even on a Monday morning. They may be amazed that you actually turn up on time, that you treat your secretary with courteous consideration and neither like a dictating machine on the one hand nor a mistress on the other. You will get your leg pulled, and your good humor and patience will count for a lot. They will expect from you a standard of behavior they do not expect from others. What a compliment that is to your Master! Your honesty in little things will be watched. Although the practice of "borrowing things" from the firm may be universal, although going home half an hour early when being paid overtime may be done by all the rest, it hardly squares with your Christian profession, and your friends will be quick to point this out.

Are you an employee? Then your attitude will be to do your job not just to get your paycheck or to keep on the right side of the boss; you will be working for Jesus, and you will want to turn out work of which He could be proud. Can you imagine any shoddy workmanship coming out of His carpentry shop in Nazareth?

You employees, put your backs into the job you do for your earthly employers, not only trying to please them when they are watching you, but all the time; do it willingly because of your love for the Lord and your desire to please him. Work hard and cheerfully in all you do, as men who are working for the Lord and not merely for the bosses, remembering that it is the Lord Christ who is going to pay you, giving you abundant wages from all he owns (Col. 3:23–24).

Are you an employer? Then your attitude to your workforce will not be to see how much profit you can get out of them and how cheaply you can make wage settlements. No, "you bosses must be scrupulously just and fair to all your employees. Always remember that you too have a Master in heaven" (Col. 4:1). When both sides of industry relate beyond themselves to the Lord and what He would want, then you get real harmony in a firm. But when He is left out and rival policies of greed govern business and industry, then it is not surprising that intransigence, suspicion, and hostility often result.

Concern for Others

One of the most distinctive Christian qualities is love for other people. This sounds trite, but it is not. It is unique—so much so that the New Testament writers had to coin a new word for it. For it is an attitude that came into the world with Jesus Christ. The ancients knew all about *philia*, "friendship," which was determined by the mutual attraction, affection, and respect of two people for each other— it depended on the worthiness of the beloved. They also knew all about *erōs*, "passionate love," and rated it as highly as we do; here again, the worthiness of the beloved was crucial. But what Jesus brought with Him was *agapē*, and that love is determined by the generosity of the giver, not the worthiness of the object. Indeed, John tells us that God so loved the world (which He assuredly could not like, feel attracted to, or respect—still less could He feel passionate emotion toward) that He gave His only Son for us.

This love was sheer self-giving. It was determined not by the worthiness of the beloved but by the nature of the Lover. He loves us not because we are lovable but because He is love. His love, like His sun, shines equally upon the just and the unjust. Now that love has reached us. That love has taken root in us and must get through us to others. Therefore, we shall care for people whether or not they are nice or attractive. We may not like them, but we shall love them, as He loves them through us. This means that we shall not make fun of the little man in the office who is the butt of everyone else's joke; we shall not allow our weeds to blow into the next-door neighbor's garden, however unneighborly he is toward us. We shall not write someone off because he went to a private school— or because he didn't. We shall not stick exclusively to people of our own social group or our own color. There will be no trace of snobbery or race discrimination in our behavior toward other people. God made them as they are. Christ loved them enough to die for them. And He wants to channel His love toward them through us.

Service Abroad

One of the ways you might consider showing this self-giving love for others, if you are young enough, is to offer to one of the missionary societies to work without pay for a year or two in a developing country overseas. You would be giving your youthful enthusiasm and such skills as you have, and you'd be doing it for Jesus. In the doing, you would be tremendously blessed and enriched yourself. Even a short period is much better than nothing. Many Christian university students spend the summer vacation in some sort of voluntary service in a developing country. Doctors in training do their electives in mission hospitals. But you don't have to be young or go overseas to find opportunities for service. There are plenty of them in your own town, your own street. The Lord will show you where you can be useful if you are open to His suggestions.

Love in the Church

One side of this love for others is stressed above all else in the New Testament. It is the very special love Christians have for other members of the Lord's family. "Love of the brotherhood and sisterhood," they call it. It is a remarkable and most moving thing. I know nothing on earth to match it. The fact that the same Lord has loved you, the same Father accepted you into His family, the same Spirit lives in you, the same motivation grips you—why, this binds you to other members of the Jesus family wherever they may be, in a way no words can describe.

I have experienced it in Cape Town and Nairobi,

in Toronto and Hong Kong, in Sydney and Accra. It is a deep sense of mutual belonging to the Lord. It means you can relate quickly to the other Christian; it means you want to give to him; it means you love to pray together; it means the two of you are prepared to stand together even if to do so is politically dangerous or socially frowned on. The church of Christ transcends all our barriers of race, age, class, and color. We must keep it that way!

3. PERSONAL RELATIONSHIPS FOR CHRIST

It goes without saying that as Christians we will want our lives to count for Jesus Christ. Magnetized by His love, we shall want to magnetize others. Let me make a few suggestions as to how we may go about this in our relationships with other people.

Demonstration Method

Without doubt this is the most telling way of all. Our lives are very often the only gospel any of our friends will read, and if the writing they see there is unattractive, they won't want to know any more. On the other hand, if they are attracted by what they see, it will not be difficult to lead them to Jesus Christ, the Author of the transformation that has impressed them. I remember an Olympic swimmer who, after a tough battle with herself, committed her life to Christ. She had been amazed by the Christian life of a friend of hers, and this disposed her to listen to the good news about Jesus.

You don't need to have been a Christian more than a few days to begin influencing people by this demonstration method. But it is sadly possible, if you cramp the Holy Spirit away in some forgotten corner of your life, to be a Christian of sorts for years without anybody noticing much difference or being attracted to Jesus Christ. And when that happens, it is more than a tragedy. It is a slander on the name of Jesus

Contribution Method

There is another way in which we can help our friends and those whom we don't even know. And that is by giving. It may be giving our time to planning a radio program or helping get a hall ready for a Christian meeting. It may be providing the refreshments at a home meeting. It may be giving our minds to planning an evangelistic meeting in the youth group. It may be buying Christian books to give or lend to others.

One man wrote to me some time ago to say that he had come to faith largely through a Christian paperback. He wrote, "You may be amused to hear that when I told a friend of my conversion his comment was, 'Oh, that's nothing. Old So-and-So found it so useful that he bought fifty copies to distribute to his friends!'" That man was using the contribu-

tion method in order to try to share his relationship
with the Lord among his friends.

But the most obvious and basic aspect of the contribution method is financial giving—giving to
Christian enterprises that you know are committed
to declaring the good news. This means informed,
discriminating, prayerful giving. Jesus once spoke
about a crooked businessman who was discovered
by his boss and fired. But before he left, he went
around to his boss's creditors and reduced their bills
for them. This meant, of course, that when he was
kicked out, he had collected a number of addresses
where he would be a welcome visitor, on account of
the financial help he had given them. Jesus commended the man for his shrewdness (though not for
his honesty!) and wished that Christians were as
farseeing in their use of their money. "Make friends
by the wise use of your money, so that when the day
of money is over there will be people to welcome
you into an eternal home," He said (Luke 16:9). In
other words, invest cash in evangelism. Through it,
some may hear and respond to the gospel who
would have remained ignorant of it, had it not been
for your sacrificial giving.

Subterranean Method

There is a fascinating verse in Paul's second letter
to the Corinthians where he invites their prayerful
support for his work of making the gospel known.
Literally he says, "You also helping together under-

neath in prayer" (2 Cor. 1:11). What could he have in mind? I suggest that he is thinking of the fortresses that were such a common feature in the ancient world. Evangelism involves storming strongholds like that in people's lives. But a frontal assault is often useless. What is needed is a tunnel. That requires hard work, sustained work, teamwork. Such work is unseen and unsung. But it is crucial if the fortress is to be taken. Prayer is like that. It assails the inner recesses of a person's will in a way that all our talking cannot.

Now let me confess to you at once that I am not much good at this. By temperament I would much rather storm walls than tunnel away in prayer. But I know, I know from constant experience, that the tunneling counts. I recall vividly a mission to Cambridge University some years back. We had seen large numbers attending night after night, between eight hundred and twelve hundred. But there was not much to show for it in terms of definite conversions. We were driven back to fundamentals, back to the tunneling of prayer. Much of the last-but-one night of that mission was given to prayer by people all over Cambridge. On the final night of the mission we had a remarkable breakthrough by the Holy Spirit of God, and many people responded to Christ, then and in the weeks that followed. It taught me once again that prayer is perhaps the most important aspect of evangelism, and the one I, at any rate, am most liable to miss out on.

Invitation Method

If one sixteen-year-old schoolboy had not used the invitation method with me, I very much doubt whether I would be writing this. He invited me to a meeting where I discovered what a Christian life was all about. As I went along regularly for many weeks, I observed the other teenagers at work on the demonstration method. And I know now that there were people in the background tunneling away on the subterranean method. These factors, under God's good hand, combined to bring me to my knees. My friend who invited me had himself only discovered Christ a few weeks previously. He was very inexperienced. But he could say, "Come and see." And I shall always be thankful that he did.

That is precisely what you find people doing in the first chapter of John's gospel. "Come and see," says Jesus to the first pair of disciples. One of them goes home in excitement and says, in effect, to his brother, Simon Peter, "Come and see." Shortly afterward we come across a skeptical Nathanael. Philip counters his hesitations with precisely the same invitation, "Come and see."

The point is obvious enough. William Temple put it crisply:

It is quite futile saying to people, "Go to the Cross." We must be able to say "Come to the Cross." And there are only two voices which can issue the invitation with effect. One is the voice of the sinless Redeemer, with which we cannot speak. And one is the voice of the forgiven sinner, who knows himself forgiven. That is our part.

It does not require long experience. It does not require the ability to explain the good news. But it does require us to have found Jesus for ourselves. And it does require the desire to share Him with others. Given those conditions, we will pluck up courage to ask people to the supper party, the house meeting, the church service, the rally, or what have you where we know the gospel will be attractively and relevantly made known. The speaker on these occasions might be the archangel Gabriel for all I care. He could do nothing whatsoever unless some faithful Christians had been doing a good job on the invitation method. And remember, they'll come if they like you, if they respect you, and if they are impressed by the changes Christ has effected in you. But if they see no difference in you, they are not likely to respond to your invitation.

Testimonial Method

It's not difficult to go one stage further than the invitation method, even when you are very green in the Christian life. It is to give Jesus a testimonial. To be willing to say, "Yes, there is a difference in my life, and it is due to Jesus. I have discovered that He is alive." Something quite simple like that. "Make Christ supreme in your heart, and then if anybody asks you the reason for your confident belief, be ready to tell him, and do it in a gentle and respectful way" (1 Pet. 3:15)—that was Simon Peter's advice. And he had had quite a bit of experience at it by the time he wrote those words.

I love that passage in the story of the Samaritan woman who had encountered Jesus. She was so thrilled that she left her water pot by the well (oblivious of the fact that she had come to draw water in the first place!), rushed back to the village, and gave Jesus an open and glowing testimonial. "Come and meet a man," she said, "who told me everything I ever did. Can this be the Christ?" The men were impressed by her testimony. They determined to find out, and after Jesus had spent a couple of days in their village, they were convinced. "Now we believe," they told the woman—and how she must have thrilled to see the fruit her testimony had borne—"because we have heard him for ourselves, not just because of what you told us. He is indeed the Savior of the world" (John 4:29, 42).

It is difficult to overestimate the effectiveness of even the most halting testimonial to Jesus given by the most recent believer. In a parish mission in East Anglia one young man (a local villager to his toenails), who came from a grim home, was led to the Savior on the morning of the last Sunday. That same evening he had the courage to get up in church and say a single brief sentence: "I have today asked Jesus Christ into my life." They all knew him, of course. He worked in the nearby slaughterhouse.

His words made more impact than the sermon—
such is the power of the testimonial method of
reaching people for Christ. It is available for every
one of us to use.

Conversation Method

How did Jesus reach men like Nicodemus and
Zacchaeus? Not by preaching a sermon to them, but
by engaging them naturally in conversation. This is
something we shall want to become adept at. It is
rewarding; it is stimulating; it is challenging; and it
is humbling. What a *reward* when you see someone
else, perhaps someone you have prayed over and
cared about for ages, commit his life to Jesus. What
a *stimulus* to you mentally and spiritually when you
have to think your way around the gospel and the
common objections to it so as to be able to share it
effectively when opportunity offers—and offer it
you may, even when you sit down next to a stranger
on the bus. The *challenge* comes from the complete
honesty we must demonstrate—the willingness to
strip away every shred of pretense and really to put
ourselves out for the other person, even if it means
shortage of food or sleep, or months of waiting and
battling in prayer. And it is *humbling* because, when
you stop to think of it, it is just fantastic that God
should use the likes of you and me to, as Paul put it,
"open blind eyes, to turn men from darkness to light
and from the power of Satan to God" (Acts 26:18).
But it happens. He does it, not you (once you start

thinking you are rather good at this evangelism business you will be useless; God cannot and will not use a proud person). But although He does it, He expects the cooperation of our lips. The Lord of glory stoops to cooperate with us!

I always feel that a splendid object lesson in evangelism by conversation is given to us by Philip, the businessman from Caesarea turned evangelist. We find his story in Acts 8. A modest man—why, he was the preacher in a great revival in Samaria; and yet, when he felt God was calling him to go down to the desert, to the desert he went, even though there would have been red faces from his team when he failed to turn up to preach to the waiting hundreds that evening! God had a job for him: an appointment with a single individual in the desert.

Philip spotted this man riding in his chariot, and such was his enthusiasm that he *run* after it. Just imagine him running after a chariot in the desert at a temperature of 140 degrees in the sun! Had anyone been around to notice him, they would have thought he was mad. But he wasn't mad. He was obedient to the leading of God. And he found (as you will find) that God had already prepared the way.

Of all incredible things, this Ethiopian in his chariot was reading not the *Jerusalem Echo* but the book of Isaiah. Better still, he was reading that piece about the Servant of the Lord who was led as a sheep to the slaughter and did not open His mouth before the shearers. What a chance! Even so, Philip did not rush in tactlessly. He asked if he could be of any help to the gentleman.

The man in the chariot asked if he could assist him over a difficulty he had with the meaning of the passage. Not surprisingly, Philip was invited into the chariot, and he began to tell the inquiring Ethiopian official about the Jesus to whom this prophecy looked forward. Before long the man professed his belief and took the opportunity of being baptized in the only pool of water in that hot, deserted Gaza strip—a spring that is still there today.

Now you and I won't expect to find people reading Isaiah 53 each time we talk to them! Nor will instant baptisms often occur. But if we ask our Friend to guide our conversations each day, and to give us opportunities to speak on His behalf when He wishes, we are in for an exciting time. He will certainly take us at our word; opportunities will come our way. We shall fail sometimes. Sometimes we shall make a little headway. Sometimes we shall get stumped by a difficulty to which we do not know the answer, and we will have to go away and find out. Sometimes, however, we shall have the joy of leading an inquirer to Jesus personally. And I know no greater joy in life than that. It is the crowning thrill of using our relationships as channels of His love. And every Christian is meant to engage in it. Don't rob yourself of blessing by holding back!

8

NEW SOCIETY

1. ON BEING THE CHURCH

We have thought a good deal so far about the individual Christian. But God is not merely concerned with the salvation of the individual. He wants to forge new individuals together into a new community, which will in turn affect society, and indeed the very cosmos we live in.

There is an increasing tendency in many countries today toward centralizing power in the hands of the government. People want to exert external constraints (be they political repression or financial involvement) to make others conform to a predetermined pattern that they have not chosen.

What Jesus wants to do is quite different. It is to change people from the *inside*, and to do it not through constraining them but through setting them free from themselves and filling them with His love for others. His strategy is to change society by transforming individuals one by one, and uniting them into a dynamic counterculture.

Celestial Strategy

When you commit yourself to Jesus Christ in personal allegiance, you join a worldwide family of those who have done the same thing. It is a family in which, according to the New Testament's very bold language, Jesus is the elder brother and we are adopted alongside Him into God's household of faith. What a wonderful conception that is! No barriers of race, class, sex, or age. That is what we are called into. Of course, we do not achieve it all at once. Indeed, we do not fully achieve it on this earth at all. But the whole thrust of New Testament ethics says to us: "Become in practice what in Christ you already are." You are sons and daughters—then live like that. You are justified—then live a just life. You are washed—behave in a clean way. You are all one in Christ Jesus—show your unity in your church life. You are accepted in the Beloved—make sure you accept other members of the family.

That is the heavenly strategy. Alas, we often frustrate it by our selfish tactics, by allowing sectional or personal interests to motivate us. We close our ears to the needs of others and remain silent when we should speak. But of the heavenly Father's plan there can be no doubt. He wants to show to the world and, indeed, Paul says, to the very angels (who have never known either the awfulness of sin or the wonder of forgiveness) what He can do with a community of people from every background and type, who commit themselves to Him and allow

Him to shape their personal and corporate lives. "God has given me the wonderful privilege of telling everyone about this plan of his," said Paul. It is "to demonstrate to the heavenly beings how perfectly wise he is, when all his family—Jews and Gentiles alike—are seen to be joined together in his church" (Eph. 3:7, 10).

The Christian Family

The church, then, is no optional extra for those who like that kind of thing. It is absolutely essential. Without it we shall not develop as Christians. Without it God's purpose will be frustrated. In the church of Christ there is available a quality of fellowship that will surpass any friendship you can find in the country club or the fitness center, or any community life shared by the dropouts. Does the New Testament not talk about our all being sheep in the one flock (John 10:16), which Christ looks after and directs; or stones in the one building that the Holy Spirit inhabits and shines out from (1 Cor. 3:16; Eph. 2:20–22; 1 Pet. 2:5)? Are we not branches in His vine (John 15:1–8), soldiers in His army (2 Tim. 2:3–4) and, incredible though it may seem, limbs in His body (Rom. 12:4–8; 1 Cor. 12:12–31)? It is impossible to exaggerate the corporate nature of the Christian life. It stares at us from every page in the New Testament. It is through this corporate life, this new society, that Jesus wants to reach the millions who are strangers to Him—not merely through the changes made in individual lives here and there.

Alas, many Christians have not seen this. I once talked to someone who had been a believer in Jesus and a fearless witness for Him at work for three years without linking up with any Christian community. He realized what he had been missing; the church, too, had missed him. It is tragic when Christians fail to see that they belong together and need each other; as a result they tend to lose their zeal because of isolation, and the church loses their freshness and warmth.

The Body of Christ

Think for a moment about that metaphor of the church being Christ's body on earth today. It speaks of the necessity and interdependence of all the different limbs in the body. It points to the harmony and unity of purpose that should characterize their relationships. It reminds us that all the members are at the disposal and direction of the mind; and that the mind can express itself only through the limbs. In other words, your ascended and invisible "mind," Jesus Christ, *needs* you, together with other members of the new society, in order to express Himself to the world through the harmony and variety of the whole body's corporate life. If you are missing from your place in the family gatherings, the whole family is impoverished and weakened. And so are you. Regular Christian companionship is absolutely necessary for mature Christian discipleship.

So join up with your local church if you have not already done so. Even if they seem ineffectual, you belong with them. By all means see what you can do to blow away the stuffiness. But you may well find that they have as much, or more, to give you as you have to give them. After all, they are more experienced members of the same family.

Church Renewal

But what if the local church seems to you to be dying? You still belong, just as you do to the more antique members of your family, the great-aunts and so on! It is very interesting to notice the way God has worked down the ages. You can see it happening time and again in the history of Israel. God does not scrap His church when it goes down the drain (as it has made a habit of doing from time to time; it is composed, after all, of sinful men and women). He doesn't throw it aside and start again. No, as Jeremiah learned down in the potter's house, God is like a potter who remolds the lump of refractory clay when it gets spoiled (Jer. 18:1–23). He does not throw it away. The church of Ezekiel's day was like a valley full of the dry bones of a dead army. But God did not say, "Right, we'll start again." In his vision, Ezekiel saw God breathe His Spirit into those dry bones, and new life soon showed itself (Ezek. 37:1–28). He continues to work like that.

Perhaps He wants to use you, among others, to revive the sleepy church in your area. Time and again a church whose minister has lost his vision and whose congregation has lost what Keith Miller calls "the taste of new wine" has been revived by one or two people who mean business with God. They have not separated themselves from their local church in search of one more lively miles away. They have heard the call to join God's people where they live, and their coming has meant renewal.

Of course, in the early days of your membership in the new society you will be in great need of building up. Therefore, you will be particularly dependent upon the warm fellowship and sound teaching of a church that knows how to care for new believers and how to build a community on the New Testament pattern. Perhaps you should go there once a week for your own soul's good; and go to the local church once a week in order to show the flag! Then later you can transfer your regular membership to where it is most needed. God will show you if you make it a matter of prayer. But don't be surprised if He calls you to join the branch of the family that is operating where you live. Give it a try, at all events, and get fully involved, not merely in public worship but in the smaller, informal meetings appropriate to your age and particular interests.

The Service Jesus Left Us

At the heart of Christian fellowship lies the Holy Communion, Eucharist, Mass, Lord's Supper—call it what you will. Incidentally, each name stresses one side of the central act of Christian devotion. *Holy Communion* reminds us that we come there to deepen our communion and fellowship with a holy God and with other members of His family. *Eucharist* means "thanksgiving" and warms our hearts with gratitude for all Christ has done to bring us into the family. *Mass* probably means either "meal" or "dismissal" of those who are not baptized into Christ—this intimate family meal is for believing members of the family and none others. And *Lord's Supper* reminds us who is the host and celebrant at that meal, Jesus Himself, the One who inaugurated it at the last supper He had with His disciples on earth.

We come then, looking back to the cross—the cross He was going to when He had that supper with them. He told them, as He broke the bread, that His body would be broken for them; He told them, as He distributed the cup, that His blood would be shed for them (Matt. 26:26–28). It happened the very next day. How we need to go back time and again to Calvary with grateful hearts in order to reappropriate the forgiveness Christ won for us there! That is where our adoption certificate into the family was issued, where our citizen rights in the new society were secured, at such tremendous cost. The Communion awakens us afresh to the awfulness of sin, the greatness of His sacrifice, and the wonder of our forgiveness.

We should also approach the Communion with a good long look at our own lives in the light of that love of Christ's. How far do we come short of His considerateness, love, purity, and honesty? Now is the time to search our consciences, to get right with Him, and as we stretch out our empty hands for the bread and the wine, symbols of His self-giving, to remember that we are indeed empty in ourselves; we deserve no good thing from God. We come simply by right of His generous free invitation to receive what He offers us—Himself.

A third side to the Holy Communion is this. The early Christians knew that "the Lord is at hand." It was no festival in honor of a dead Jesus, but a meal of companionship with a risen Lord. So thank Him that He is alive, that He is at work in you and the rest of the community of the Resurrection, as the church might well be called. That is something to rejoice about.

Make a point, too, of looking around you. That older woman, that plainspoken shopkeeper, that lanky youth, that friendly bus driver—you all belong together in the Lord's family. You all kneel or sit together to receive the bread and wine, the sacred emblems of His body and His blood given without distinction for you all. No place for pride before such self-giving love, is there? No need to have any chip on the shoulder! No excuse for keeping up a feud with any other member of the same family. You are all on a par: fellow sinners, fellow heirs of the same kingdom, and fellow guests at the same table.

And spare a thought for the future God has for His new society. It may not bring in Utopia on earth.

God never said it would. But each Lord's Supper should have a touch of the future glory about it. It should remind us of the marriage supper of the Lamb (as the book of Revelation picturesquely calls it), the final consummation in joyous harmony of God's plan for all His people. *"Maranatha!"* cried the earliest Christians in their native Aramaic when they sat at the Lord's Table. "O Lord, come!" (1 Cor. 16:22; cf. Rev. 22:20). It is as if they said, "Lord, You have come to this world, and lived and died for us. You have set us in this new society. We see many marks of Your presence and of Your renewing work. But, Lord, there's such a long way to go. Hasten the day when You wind up Your plans for this world, and bring us all to the family table in heaven." No escapism, there, you will notice. But just a foretaste of the future glory to give us perspective in our daily work and the determination to be the best for Him on earth.

Make room, then, for informal fellowship at home and at work; make room for meeting other Christians, especially on Sunday; make room for services of other kinds; but whatever you do, do not neglect Holy Communion. It is the seal of your pardon, the food for your Christian life, the bond of your fellowship, and the foretaste of heaven.

Corporate Worship

Although Holy Communion is perhaps the most important act of Christian worship and fellowship—

it was, after all, instituted by Christ Himself—it is not the only one. The early Christians found it so important to meet together both formally and informally for mutual encouragement and service, for worship and prayer, for learning and sharing, that they broke the imperial law to do it and were prepared to face execution rather than give it up. That is how highly they rated the fellowship of the new society. "We ought to see how each of us may best arouse others to love and active goodness, not staying away from church meetings, as some do, but rather encouraging one another, and all the more so as the day of Christ's return is drawing nearer"— such was the advice given in the letter to the Hebrews (10:24–25). The quality of discipleship that that fellowship engendered captured the Roman world. Ancient paganism had nothing to compare with the loving, useful, happy lives of the Christian communities in their midst. And modern paganism has nothing to compare with it, either.

But if the church is to make that kind of impact in society, its worship must have, and be seen to have, three qualities. Without them, what is done in church becomes as empty and meaningless as a shell when the nut has been removed. Worship must be united, it must be shared, and it must issue in practical goodness.

1. Real worship must be united. Naturally, for the various limbs in the body are stretching up in unison to praise and thank and trust and learn from their head. But if it is well known that the minister can't bear the organist, that the choir eats candy and plays games through the sermon, that the congregation never talk to each other afterward, and that the church council meetings always develop into an unholy quarrel between the minister and one of the members—well, it is hardly surprising if such a church cuts no ice with the neighborhood. It is useless preaching a gospel of reconciliation if it is perfectly obvious that the members of the church have not settled their differences. And that goes for denominations as well as churches. We all know that Roman Catholics have for centuries unchurched all other Christians but are now changing their tune. It has been equally true that many Protestants have unchurched all Roman Catholics and have thought it impossible that people should continue as members of that church once they had come to a living faith in Jesus. This Protestant exclusivism is as wrong as the Roman Catholic intransigence was. Every believer in Jesus is baptized by the one Spirit into the one body of Christ, in which there is no essential difference between Protestant or Roman Catholic, black or white Work for that unity in your place of worship.

2. Real worship must be shared. The Lord does not expect us to file into an ancient monument once a week, try to cope with Elizabethan English, marvel at Gothic architecture and a choir in resplendent clothes, and listen to a professional at a lectern. Where these conditions still persist, the church has to change. There needs to be room for the mutual enrichment and encouragement of different members of the body. It simply will not do for one member to monopolize the service. There has to be room for the discussion of Christian principles and their outworking in daily life, not just passive listening to a sermon from the preacher, however talented the person may be. (This is not to knock the sermon; there must be proclamation of God's truth, no less than discussion of how to apply it. The two belong together.) There has to be informal discussion in the small group as well as in the Sunday service to enable the members to get to know, trust, and learn from one another.

3. *Real worship must be practical.* It has to issue in "love and active goodness," as the writer to the Hebrews reminded us. Genuine caring for the needs of society must be evident. It may be the quiet visiting of people who are sick, or reading to people with mobility impairments. It may be mounting a campaign for better housing or for children's play areas. "Fellowship is all very well," remarked one friend to whom I showed this manuscript in an earlier draft, "but the dying, hungering, longing people on the housing estate [public housing] or in the lecture room alongside me remain dying. We are damned if our lives are not pinned on that cross with our Lord. James rightly says that 'faith' alone is useless: faith is not faith when it draws back before the sacrificial giving of everything we have and are." He rightly points out the great disinclination to *work* among Christian people; we prefer to take

refuge in a cozy little Bible study. But the two are intertwined. We shall only increase in understanding when we obey Christ and engage in loving, active service for Him. Otherwise we shall find dullness and apathy at the weekly Bible study when the group meets and has to admit, "Sorry we haven't actually managed to be the hands and feet of Jesus today, but bless us all the same!" Genuine worship and genuine work go hand in hand. They cannot be separated if either is to remain healthy.

Is worship a priority in your church? Is it united? Is it relevant? Is there scope for all to take a real part? Does it lead to action? If not, start stirring things up. It should be.

2. ON BEING THE CHURCH IN THE WORLD

Club for Nonmembers

The new society must never degenerate into an introspective club. It is, in the memorable words of Archbishop Temple, the only society in the world that exists for the benefit of those who are not members.

Christians will therefore be concerned not only with evangelism, which we have considered in a previous chapter, but with social and political issues, with the equitable distribution of wealth and power, and with the preservation of our world for future generations. There is a great deal that

Christians can do in these areas. The church should assuredly not leave politics to the politicians or economics to the economists. The church at large, and the individual Christian in particular, may not be well equipped in any detail to pronounce on these highly complicated issues. But we all have some influence. We can stand up and speak up when the will of Christ is plain. It is our duty as Christian citizens. And in so doing we shall undoubtedly affect society. Let us take a glance at some of the crucial areas where as Christians we should be involved.

Social Concern

I remember being delighted, on a visit to Australia, to discover the tremendous social conscience of the diocese of Sydney. It has the reputation of being the most uniformly evangelical diocese in the whole Anglican communion. Far from evangelistic emphasis being the foe of social involvement, the reverse is proved to be the case. It gives more money to social work than any diocese in the world, and the motivation comes directly from a strong sense of the new life brought by Christ. Therefore, *of course* the church must build hospitals for older people, villages for retired people, homes for unmarried mothers, boys and girls on probation, and people when they come out of prison. *Of course* they must provide help for destitute people and would-be suicides. It is as important as the missionary work in which they engage so wholeheartedly.

Sydney's Archbishop Marcus Loane was a superb example of this balance. On the one hand, he had just walked the fabulously wild Kadoka Trail, a route through the mountains and jungles that had a gruesome reputation in the Second World War, in order to help raise a million dollars for the impov-erished diocese of New Guinea. On the other hand, he had just fearlessly accused the federal govern-ment of policies producing a hundred thousand unemployed and family hardship hurting half a million. Angry questions were asked in Parliament. One member requested the archbishop to stick to sin while politicians handled economics. The prime minister patronizingly said he would have a chat with the archbishop, who clearly did not under-stand these things. The result? Churchmen at large backed the Christian lead given by Archbishop Loane, and all the other diocesan bishops backed him to the hilt, to the great embarrassment of a government unwilling to grapple with a crying so-cial problem because of a forthcoming election. Christian concern over the unemployment issue led to a national inquiry into the causes and cure of poverty in Australia.

Race Relations

A word about race relations may not be out of place in a day when, sadly, they are often a major disruptive force in societies across the world.

Many years ago in America a Civil Rights Commission came out in support of claims by black people for equality in citizenship rights, and yet absolutely nothing was done to carry those recommendations through. The magnetic leadership of Martin Luther King, Jr., with his policy of nonviolent protest allied to civil disobedience, forced both president and Congress to act. Though assassinated in the cause of winning justice for black people, Martin Luther King's life and ideals still live on and have influenced the cause of freedom the world over. In his Christmas Eve broadcast, shortly before he was killed, he outlined his vision for humanity. It shows not only the greatness of the man but the Christ-centered motivation for his social concern:

I still have a dream this morning that one day every Negro in the country, every colored person in the world, will be judged on the basis of the content of his character rather than the color of his skin, and every man will respect the dignity and worth of human personality. I still have a dream today that one day the idle industries of Appalachia will be revitalized and the empty stomachs of Mississippi will be filled, and brotherhood will be more than a few words at the end of a prayer, but rather the first item on every legislative agenda. I still have a dream today that one day justice will roll down like water, and righteousness like a mighty stream. I still have a dream today that in all of our state houses and city halls men will be elected to go there who will do justly, and love mercy and walk humbly with their God. I still have a dream today that one day war will come to an end, that men will beat their swords into plowshares and their spears into pruning hooks, that nations will no longer rise up against nations, neither will they study war any more. . . . I still have a dream that with this faith we shall be able to adjourn the councils of despair and bring new light into the dark chambers of pessimism. With this faith we will be able to speed up the day when there will be peace on earth and goodwill toward men. It will be a glorious day, the morning stars will sing together, and the sons of God will shout for joy.

Such was the vision behind the practical action of one of this century's truly great Christians. Yet he was shot. Does this mean that Christians are mistaken in renouncing force and rejecting violent revolution in a world that seems to be becoming increasingly violent?

Revolutionary Violence

This is a difficult issue. It is hard, on the one hand, to see how the church, committed as it is to love and peace, could be involved in violence and revolution. But what is it to do, on the other hand, when the surrounding society is utterly corrupt, justice has been banished, and oppression is the order of the day? The temptation to violence is almost irresistible in these circumstances, and yet for the life of me I cannot see violent revolution squaring with the example of Jesus. Though He had some Zealot revolutionaries among His disciples, He would not accept the option of violent revolution in the interests of either nation or ideology. Ironically enough, He was crucified as a revolutionary leader ("King of the Jews"), and yet He refused to allow the ideological cause of the kingdom of God or the political cause of throwing off the Roman yoke to tempt Him to sanction arms. Force is not exorcised by force. Violence breeds violence. And that will give the Christian pause before considering it, even under extreme provocation. For the cross of Jesus shows us clearly that violence is disarmed not by retaliation but by patient, innocent suffering.

There have been Christians of the utmost spirituality and integrity who, goaded beyond endurance, have accepted the option of violence for the sake of helping other people whom it seemed impossible to defend in any other way. One thinks of Camilo Torres, the Roman Catholic priest, who was so appalled at the conditions of the peasants in Colombia that he sided with the guerrillas in the mountains in the attempt to improve their lot by violent revolution. This brave man joined the revolution out of love for his neighbor, and we must salute him. He was shot in action in 1966. And many Latin American billboards carried the legend *Camilo viva!* for years afterward.

Or one thinks of Dietrich Bonhoeffer, the lifelong Christian pacifist, who eventually was so appalled by the atrocities of Hitler's Germany that he took part, out of Christian love for the German people, in an attempt to kill Hitler—and paid the extreme penalty.

These great men reluctantly took the way of violence, but only when, evil as they saw it to be, it seemed less evil than the status quo. They may have been wrong. But we certainly cannot judge them. They had the courage to give practical proof of their sense of justice and their Christian love for others, knowing that they were risking their lives by so doing. Equally great men, such as Martin Luther King in the United States, Bishop Helder Camara in Brazil, and Bishop Wilson in a Japanese prisoner of war camp in World War II, have followed Jesus in meeting violence by suffering, and in the long run their judgment may well prove the sounder. "Christians," said Jacques Ellul, at the end of his careful book *Violence*, "will be sufficiently and completely present in the world if they suffer with those who suffer, if they seek out with those sufferers the one way of salvation, if they bear witness before God and man to the consequences of injustice and the proclamation of love."

Reactionary Violence

But there is a reactionary as well as a revolutionary violence. In the South American scene, reactionary violence is understandably sparked by the violent oppression, rapacity, and ruthlessness of the tiny ruling class. In South Africa, the black majority has for many years been shamelessly maltreated and kept down by the wealthy white minority. In Eastern Europe, it has been the same story as Communist regimes have silenced all opposition with the gun and with the gulag. What attitude is the Christian to adopt?

It is tempting to join the guerrillas and match violence with violence. But that is not Christ's ideal for us. The way of reactionary violence is bound to fall apart from its own dynamics of hate. We have seen that happen with graphic suddenness in Eastern Europe in 1989. The only thing in the world that will last is love. And love is the political option that has for so long remained untried. Michael Cassidy wrote a fascinating book in 1990 entitled *The Politics of Love*, where he applied these four principles of love in politics with clarity and power to the South African scene that he knows so well, and where he has for so long been a powerful advocate for the ways of Christ. Here are his four "laws of love":

Love sees politics as all about people.
Love deals with its own heart first.
Love loves, humanizes, and forgives its enemy.
Love hears and sees the other side.

Whether the people of South Africa will heed this powerful appeal remains to be seen. But there can be no other cure for violence, reactionary or revolutionary. The only way to change your enemy is to love him: it is costly, sacrificial, humbling, but the only way, so Jesus tells us. He ought to know. He trod it Himself.

The Environment

In recent years, leading scientists the world over have been warning us that unless we change our priorities radically, the earth is heading for destruction within two generations. The threat to human survival comes from a variety of sources. There is the specter of the hydrogen bomb; and an increasing number of nations join the Nuclear Club every year. There is the stockpiling by many nations of germ weapons that can wipe out a whole country overnight. There is the unsolved problem of hunger; nearly two-thirds of the world's population is underfed. There is the appalling threat of overpopulation. The world population took two centuries to double between the seventeenth century and the nineteenth century. But now it doubles every thirty years! By the year 2000 there will be twice as many people on this overcrowded planet as there were in the seventies. Most of them will be born to starvation, since food supplies cannot even support the present population, and almost all the cultivable land in the world has already been used up.

There are plenty of other problems. We are depleting the natural resources of our planet at a shattering rate and cutting down the rain forests. Furthermore, the world is being polluted to an incredible extent, and the ozone layer is eroding at an alarming rate. We are like rats, fouling our own cage. We pollute the atmosphere with carbon dioxide, poison the seas with oil and chemicals, and inundate the land with garbage.

Add to this the gross inequality between the haves and the have-nots and the critical nature of the world situation comes into even sharper focus. Americans eat fifty times more food in a lifetime than do people in India. The inequality between industrialized and nonindustrialized nations to so marked a degree is a massive irritant to war.

As Christians whose lot it is to live in such a significant and indeed terrible chapter of the world's history, how are we to carry out the Lord's command to love our neighbor? Bishop Hugh Montefiore, who has consistently pointed out the seriousness of these issues, wrote this selective adaptation of the Ten Commandments:

I am the Lord your God; you shall have no other gods but me.

You shall not make to yourself any graven image or idol, such as the Gross National Product or possessions or riches, *whether in the heavens above or in the earth beneath or in the waters under the earth: you shall not bow down and serve them.*

You shall not take the name of the Lord your God in vain by calling on his name but ignoring his natural law.

Remember that you set apart one day in the week

for true festivity, or you will be bored stiff in the technological age you are bringing on yourselves.

Honour your father and mother, but do not seek to prolong their natural term of life so that they are miserable.

You shall not murder future generations by your present greed.

You shall not commit sexual sin by producing more children than is your right.

You shall not bear false witness against your overseas neighbours by lying to yourself about the extent of their needs.

You shall not covet an ever-increasing standard of living.

Secular Assumptions—and Christian Attitudes

As Christians, we shall want to contest the assumptions of most of our contemporaries in the industrialized West; namely, that we have a right to an ever-increasing standard of living, that increased wealth brings increased happiness, that governments should make material prosperity their chief aim, and that people are autonomous over the environment. We believe that we are not autonomous here on this earth, but responsible to the God who put us here for our stewardship of the resources of His world. We believe that we are interdependent with the natural world, of which we are a part, and that flouting natural ecological law will destroy the world and ourselves. We believe that happiness does not lie in the multitude of things that we possess; it is not wealth but relationships that bring the greatest joy. We believe that this world is not the be-all and end-all of life but the foretaste of eternity, and our readiness for God's future will be determined by the way we have lived here on earth.

Our character is the only thing we can take out of this life with us—and our character is developed by the responsible choices that we make on just such issues as those we have been discussing. We believe that nature is God's handiwork. Its beauty is His beauty, and when we spoil it, we hurt Him. We believe that we cannot love God if we do not love our neighbor; and our neighbor consists not only of poor and needy people at the other end of the world, but the generations yet unborn. We shall reflect on those principles and act on them.

Christian Attitudes

We dare not, therefore, as Christians in today's world, be bound by nationalism, by prejudice based on race, color, and class, or by considerations of personal gain. We dare not assume that because we do not see the sixty thousand homeless people sleeping at night on the streets of Bombay, we are not involved. We are involved. They are our brothers and sisters. No longer can we assume that it is our right to have an increase in income each year, a car (and preferably a new one every two years), a satellite TV, and an expensive annual holiday. It is not our right. It is salutary to recall that even the person on state assistance or Social Security in the West lives like a prince compared with the average citizen throughout the Two-Thirds World.

We Christians must show ourselves masters over the greed, selfishness, and irresponsibility that are taken for granted in our society. Our Christian allegiance must affect our pockets and our politics—no longer will it do to vote according to our class or according to what will benefit us most. We shall seek to discover which party as a whole is more committed to dealing equitably with the problems bedeviling our world; which party is committed to values beyond mere increase of wealth; which party cares most about the future of the world and about our less-fortunate neighbors in the world. And we shall vote for that party.

Workshop Here; Residence Above

"Workshop Below; Residence Above." You may have seen a notice to that effect by the doorbell of someone who lives over the shop. Well, read that in a Christian sense, and it will give a proper perspective to what has just been said. Christians ought to be very clear that no human-created society can ever be a Utopia. All Towers of Babel get short shrift in Scripture because it is made abundantly plain that any lasting building is God's work, not ours, and that the kingdom that we seek is the kingdom of heaven, not of men and women. We cannot bring it in. What we touch we spoil. The Christian hope for the future is built fairly and squarely upon God and what He will do; just as the Christian assurance about the past is built on God and what He has done through the incarnation, death, and resurrection of Jesus. Incidentally, the events that took place in Judea over nineteen hundred years ago are the pledge that we Christians are not kidding ourselves about the future. We live "in between the times," marked as they are by the first and last comings of Jesus. "God's gracious intervention, bringing rescue for all mankind, *has* appeared," writes Paul to Titus; and from the certainty of that fact in the past he can look forward with assurance to the day when "our great God and Savior, Jesus Christ, *will* appear in majesty." Christ's first coming was in humility and as Savior: "He gave himself for us in order to rescue us from every lawless way, and cleanse us as a people for his own possession, eager to do good" (Titus 2:11–14). Christ's second coming will be in majesty, no longer as Savior but as Judge, when, at the end of history, He will bring in the fullness of the kingdom that was inaugurated at His first coming to our world. We live between those two great comings. Our goal is nothing that we can construct, but as the poet who wrote the book of Revelation conceived it, in a fusion of metaphors:

The Holy City, the new Jerusalem, coming down from God out of heaven. It was a glorious sight,

beautiful as a bride at her wedding. I heard a
shout from the throne saying, "Look, the home of
God is now among men, and he will live with
them, and they will be his people; yes, God himself will be among them. He will wipe away all
tears from their eyes, and there shall be no more
death, nor sorrow, nor crying, nor pain. All of
that has gone forever" (Rev. 21:2–4 TLB)

Such is the Christian hope. It is a hope based on
the reality of the resurrection of Jesus Christ. That
does not, however, mean we are to sit and wait for
the end. Christians down through the ages have
tended to make one of two mistakes at this point.
Either they have neglected the future hope and put
all their efforts into working for an earthly Utopia,
or they have refused to get involved in the social
and political intricacies of the world of their day,
waiting for the second coming of Christ.

How different the balance of the biblical writers!
They believed passionately in the reality of God's
future, when Paradise Lost would become Paradise
Regained. But for that very reason, and imbued
with that hope, they were committed to working at
earthly problems like race and labor relations, care
for the widows, and relief for famine-stricken people. It is no coincidence that the passage I have just
quoted from Paul's letter to Titus has several
phrases between the mention of Christ's first and
second comings. They concern the life we should be
living now, in between the Advents, a life marked

by practical honesty and goodness. We Christians, therefore, should be allying ourselves with every effort that is made to increase justice, humanity, equality, and peace among people. But we should be very clear that the best humankind can achieve will be a very provisional order until the day when Christ returns to right all wrongs and bring in the fullness of His kingdom.

Meanwhile, God has given us His Holy Spirit, the first installment of heaven. Equipped with that Spirit the Christian church, the new society, has a vitally important part to play in molding the attitudes of society in the coming decades, when the destiny of the world, for doom or for deliverance, may well lie in the balance. Our lifestyle, molded by that same Holy Spirit (as we make Christ King in our individual lives and in the Christian church at large), will show that new life really is available for an old and jaded world. Life that begins now and stretches beyond the grave. Life that affects society now and culminates in the community of heaven. This life is available—for anyone who is prepared to pay the price. And though costly, it is infinitely satisfying, for it is what we were created for: to know God and enjoy Him forever.

Michael Green, formerly Principal of St. John's College, Nottingham, and for many years rector of St. Aldate's, Oxford, is currently Professor of Evangelism at Regent College, Vancouver. He is the author of more than twenty books and the editor of the I Believe series and the Jesus Library. Green received M.A. degrees from Oxford University and Cambridge University. He resides in Vancouver, British Columbia, Canada.